THE
FAR·EAST
COOKBOOK

THE

FAR·EAST
COOKBOOK

More than 175 tantalizing recipes
from the Far East

a Salamander book

Published by Salamander Books Limited
LONDON

Available at:
SULU Arts & Books
465 Sixth Street, 2nd Floor
San Francisco, CA 94103
Phone: (415) 777-2451
Fax: (415) 777-4676

a **Salamander book**

Published by Salamander Books Limited
129-137 York Way
London N7 9LG
United Kingdom

Distributed by Random House Value Publishing, Inc.
40 Engelhard Avenue
Avenel, New Jersey 07001

1 3 5 7 9 8 6 4 2

© Salamander Books Ltd. 1995

ISBN 0-517-14030-6

All correspondence concerning the content of this volume
should be addressed to Salamander Books Ltd.

Printed in Italy

CONTENTS

INTRODUCTION

The area loosely termed as the Far East, covers a vast expanse of the world. It is a fascinating area comprised of richly varied countries. There is, however, a core of similarities running through the cuisines of all the countries. They are all exciting, enticing and, to Westerners, have an exotic mystique.

They have broadly similar indigenous fruits and vegetables, rice is ubiquitous and spices are used extensively and cleverly to add zest to dishes and transform the same food so it tastes different from day to day. Spices and seasonings also have clearly defined attributes that are supposed to help the body in specific functions – ginger, for example, is considered a digestive. Throughout the region certain spices crop up time and time again, namely garlic, ginger, green onions, soy products, and chiles.

Dips, chutneys, condiments, relishes and pickles have an important role on nearly every meal table. Dairy products are not used, meat is a luxury and desserts are rarely served (meals end with fresh fruit). Emphasis is placed on balancing spicy, hot flavors with cool ones; salty or sour tastes with sweetness.

In the Far East, diners sit at round tables, and most meals (banquets are the major exception) do not follow the Western structure of separate courses. Instead, dishes tend to be served simultaneously, or simply in the order in which they are cooked. One of the most exciting aspects of Far Eastern eating is that at every meal you get what amounts to a multi-choice meal because diners dip into dishes as they choose, taking a small portion to their plates or bowls to put on a bed of rice.

Together, the cuisines of the Far East compose a beguiling collection of many of the world's most appetizing dishes, evolved over centuries. There is no need to eat only the dishes of just one country at a time. Have fun and feel free to prepare meals from whatever you fancy, juxtaposing a Japanese recipe with a Thai recipe, a Malay dish with a Chinese one, for example. However, it is best to precede a highly spiced dish with a more subtle one, not vice versa.

COOKING IN THE FAR EAST

Although there is a backbone of similarities between all the countries of the Far East, the diverse cuisines all have their own essential and unique characters.

CHINA

China is the largest of the Asian countries and it has the most varied landscape, climate and cultures. Inevitably, this has resulted in a number of different culinary styles. For example, in the north, where it is colder, wheat, not rice, is the staple and is used to make noodles, pancakes and dumplings. Dishes are more robust, and beef is more commonly eaten than elsewhere. In contrast, in the east around Shanghai, where the climate is milder, the land fertile and the seas and rivers provide fish and seafood, dishes are delicate and often slightly sweet; rice is used generously. The food of Sichuan, in the west, shows yet another contrast – the cooking is spiked with chiles and sweet-sour and salty combinations. Cantonese cooking, from the south, is linked with stir-frying, which grew out of a shortage of fuel (brief, hot cooking used less wood or coal). To be successful, stir-frying must be teamed with time-consuming chopping, slicing and dicing of the vegetables, poultry, meat or fish used in a dish.

JAPAN

Historically, Japan has remained isolated from its neighbors, so its cuisine has greater individuality. Flavors are more subtle than those of other Far Eastern countries, being typically clear, light and delicate; Japanese cooks believe that separate flavors should be shown in relief, rather than blended to a mellow whole. Harmony and balance are all-important.

Japanese dishes are characterized by elegant simplicity. Great attention is paid to the artistic, neat appearance of dishes, but not at the expense of the freshness or quality of the ingredients or the flavor of the food.

Until fairly recently, the Japanese diet was mainly a vegetarian one relieved by fish, which is still enjoyed raw as well as cooked.

KOREA

Koreans favor more pungent flavors, although their spice repertoire is fairly restricted. Garlic, chiles, gingerroot and green onions are used generously. Soy sauce, sesame oil and seeds, often toasted and crushed with salt, also make frequent appearances.

SOUTH-EAST ASIA

The countries of South-East Asia – Thailand, Malaysia, the Philippines, and Indonesia – share common flavorings beyond the Far Eastern ones – lemon grass, garlic, chiles, fermented seafood pastes and sauces. Richness in sauces comes not from dairy products but coconut milk and cream, while nuts are ground to a paste to thicken and enrich. Satays and curries are common throughout the region. Although ingredients are the same throughout South-East Asia, each country has its own way of preparing and serving them.

THAILAND

Thai dishes are made fragrant and flavorful by a glorious array of aromatics – bright galangal, tangy citrusy limes and the more subtle lemon fragrance of lemon grass, heady basil, fiery chiles, and garlic. Savory dishes are characterized by a subtle sweetness, resulting from the addition of palm sugar. The appearance of dishes matters more to Thais than to other South East Asians but Thai cuisine has the least European influence. Instead, Chinese and Indian influences are noticeable both in the cooking methods and the ingredients. But in Thai hands they have a new, sophisticated profile. Stir-fries are not thickened with cornstarch as they are in China, so are lighter and fresher tasting. Unlike Indian curries, Thai curries are cooked quickly and lack the rich heaviness that results from long slow simmering.

INDONESIA

The use of spices is a particularly notable characteristic of the Indonesian cuisine, for the famed 'Spice Islands' produce a treasure trove of exotic aromatics. Curries are important, but often the rich color and flavor of soy sauce produce a curry with a very different and distinctive taste. Sauces are also important. They may be thin and fiery, thick and nutty, oily and spicy-sweet, or any combination of the above.

Dishes may be served hot, warm or at room temperature, but usually the latter. Condiments are a must, with soy sauce, chile, shallot and seafood pastes the main ingredients of compound sauces, plus a rainbow of raw and pickled fruits and vegetables.

PHILIPPINES

The colorful cooking of the Philippine Islands is an exciting amalgam of many influences, principally Chinese, Indonesian, Malaysian and, unusually for South-East Asia, Spanish. The unique Felippino custom of 'merienda' has its roots in Spanish 'tapas', although it begins about 4 o'clock in the afternoon and combines a selection of small cakes and sweet dishes with savory snacks, often served buffet-style, as is much of the food on the islands.

There is a sharpness and tartness running through much Felippino cooking which comes from the use of a citrus fruit, the kalamansi, that is halfway between a lime and a lemon, and palm vinegar.

Bamboo shoots: Young tender shoots from the bottom of the bamboo shoots, these are crunchy but bland, absorbing stronger flavors. Sold canned. Rinse before use.

Banana leaves: Used to make containers for steamed foods, to which they impart a delicate taste.

Bean curd: Known as tofu in Japanese, this is a nutritious low-calorie food made from soy beans. Bland, with a soft-cheese texture, it absorbs other flavors. Soft bean curd is mostly used in soups and sauces.

Bean sprouts: These small, young tender shoots are usually mung beans that have germinated, although other beans can also be allowed to sprout. Bean sprouts are nutritious, containing generous amounts of vitamins and minerals, and add a delicious crunch to stir-fry dishes.

Black beans: These small, fermented soy beans are very salty. Black bean sauce, in cans or bottles, is a quick, handy substitute.

Bok choy: This mild vegetable with white stalks and dark green leaves is widely available in supermarkets.

Celery cabbage (wong ah bok): A delicate pale green vegetable with a sweet taste that makes it ideal for use in salads. Its delicate flavor blends superbly with other foods.

Chiles: Add flavor as well as 'hotness'. Thais favour small and very fiery 'bird's eye' chiles but elsewhere these are only available in Thai markets. Chiles are rarely labelled with the variety or an indication of 'hotness'; as a rule of thumb, smaller varieties are hotter than large ones. Dried chiles have a more earthy, fruity flavor. The seeds and white veins inside a chile are not only hotter than the flesh, but have less flavor, and are generally removed before using. Chiles contain an oil that can make the eyes and even the skin sting, so wash your hands after preparing them and avoid touching the eyes or mouth.

Chinese beans: The tender pods of these green beans can be eaten whole.

1 galangal; 2 gingerroot; 3 cilantro; 4 Chinese black mushrooms; 5 chiles;
6 Thai sweet basil; 7 Thai holy basil.

Snap beans or French beans can be substituted.

Chinese black mushrooms: These dried mushrooms have quite a pronounced flavor amd must be soaked for 20 to 30 minutes before use. The stalks tend to be tough so are usually discarded. Available in Oriental food stores.

Chinese black vinegar: Black vinegars are made from grains other than rice, and aged to impart complex, smoky flavors with a light, pleasant bitterness. Substitute sherry, balsamic vinegar or a good red wine vinegar.

Choy sum (Chinese flowering cabbage): Very similar to 'bok choy',

though slightly smaller, with narrower stalks and slightly paler green leaves; the distinctive feature is the yellow flowers. These are cooked with the rest of the vegetables.

Coconut cream: The layer that forms on the top of coconut milk.

Coconut milk: Not the liquid from inside a coconut, but extracted from shredded coconut flesh that has been soaked in water. Soak the shredded flesh of 1 medium coconut in 1-1/4 cups boiling water for 30 minutes. Turn into a strainer lined with muslin or cheesecloth and squeeze the cloth hard to extract as much liquid as possible. Coconut milk can also be made from unsweetened shredded coconut

soaked in boiling water, or milk, which will be richer. Allow 1-1/4 cups liquid to 2-2/3 cups shredded coconut. Put into a blender and mix for 1 minute. Refrigerate coconut milk. Ready prepared coconut milk is sold canned (which affects the flavor slightly) and in plastic containers.

Cilantro leaves: Best bought in large bunches rather than small packages. Stand whole bunches in cold water in a refrigerator.

Cilantro roots: Roots have a more muted taste than the leaves. Large cilantro bunches sold in Middle Eastern stores often include the roots. Fresh roots will last for several days if kept wrapped in the refrigerator, or can be frozen. If unavailable, use cilantro stalks.

Daikon: A long, white, bland root vegetable with a crunchy texture, also called Japanese white radish.

Fish sauce: Also called nuoc nam and nam pla, this is made from salted, fermented anchovies and used in sauces, stir-fries and as a condiment. It is rich in protein and B vitamins and is salty, but the flavor is mild. The lighter Vietnamese and Thai sauces are best. A little goes a long way. Keeps almost indefinitely.

Five-spice powder: A blend of cinnamon, cloves, star anise, fennel and Szechuan pepper, used in Chinese marinades and sauces. Sold in supermarkets and Asian markets.

Galangal: Also known as Thai ginger, laos and lengk haus. There are two varieties, lesser and greater; the latter is preferred and more likely to be found in the West. It looks similar to gingerroot but the skin is thinner, paler, more translucent and tinged with pink. Its flavor is also similar to ginger but less hot and with definite seductive citrus, pine notes. To use, peel and thinly slice or chop. The whole root will keep for up to 2 weeks if wrapped in paper and kept in the cool drawer of the refrigerator, or can be frozen. Allow to thaw just sufficiently to enable the amount required to be sliced off, then return the root to the freezer. Galangal is also sold dried as a powder or in slices, the latter giving the better flavor. Substitute 1 dried slice or 1 teaspoon powder to each 1/2 inch used in a recipe; in recipes where fresh galangal is pounded with other spices, mix the dried form in after the pounding; elsewhere, use as normal.

Gingerroot: This knobby root's sweet spicy flavor is used in oriental soups, stir-fries and in fish dishes. Choose firm, heavy pieces that have a slight sheen. To stow, wrap in paper towels, place in a plastic bag and store in the vegetable drawer of the refrigerator.

Gingko nuts: These have a hard shell, which must be removed before cooking, and a creamy colored flesh. Shelled gingko nuts are also available in cans. If unavailable, substitute almonds.

Hoisin sauce: A reddish brown sauce based on soy beans and flavored with garlic, chiles and a combination of spices. Flavors vary between brands, but it is nearly always quite sweet and it can range from the thickness of a soft jam to a runny sauce. It is used in Chinese marinades, barbecue sauces and stir-fries.

Kaffir lime leaves: The smooth, dark green leaves give an aromatic, clean citrus-pine flavor and smell. They keep well in a cool place and can be frozen. Use ordinary lime peel if kaffir lime leaves are unavailable, substituting 1-1/2 teaspoons finely grated peel for 1 kaffir lime leaf.

Lemon grass: A long, slim bulb with a lemon-citrus flavor. To use, cut off the root tip, peel off the tough outer layers and cut away the top part of stalk. The stalks will keep for several days in a cool place, or they can be chopped and frozen. If unavailable, use the grated peel of 1/2 lemon or a lime in place of 1 stalk.

Long beans: Although these can grow to over 3 feet it is best to use younger, smaller ones. Green beans can replace them.

Lychees: Canned lychees are easy to find in supermarkets, but fresh ones are now becoming far more readily

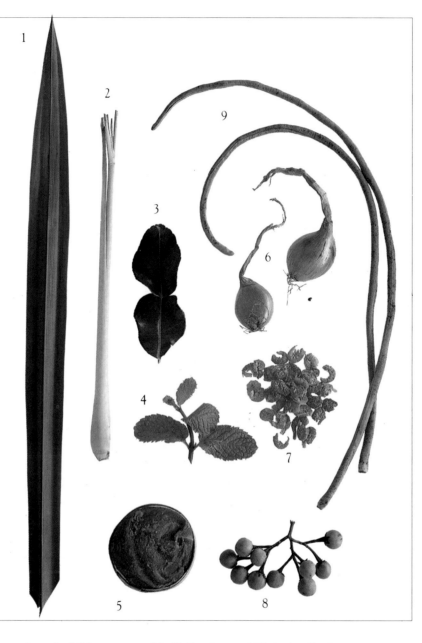

1 *pandanus leaf*; 2 *lemon grass*; 3 *kaffir lime leaves*; 4 *Thai mint*; 5 *palm sugar*; 6 *shallots*; 7 *dried shrimp*; 8 *pea eggplants*; 9 *long beans*.

available. They need no more preparation than using the fingers to easily crack the nobbly, brittle coating. Beneath it, delicious, perfumed white flesh surrounds a smooth central seed.

Mango: There are many different types of mango, each one varying in size, shape and color. Select fruit that feels heavy for its size and is free of bruises or damage. A ripe mango yields to gentle pressure and should have an enticing, scented aroma. The flesh inside should have a wonderful, luxurious and slightly exotic texture

and flavor but poor quality fruit can be disappointing; the key is the fragrance. If a mango is a little firm when bought, leave it in a warm sunny place to finish ripening.

Mushrooms: Chinese cooks seldom buy fresh mushrooms, preferring to use dried ones. These must be soaked before cooking. Put the mushrooms into a bowl, cover with boiling water, cover the bowl, leave for about 20 to 30 minutes until swollen and pliable, then drain well. If the stems are tough, discard them.

Cloud ear: Also known as 'wood ear', these are added for their texture rather than flavor, as they have little.

Straw: These thin, tall, leaflike mushrooms are also known as 'paddy straw' or 'grass' mushrooms. They are sold canned as well as dried.

Winter black mushrooms: With a fairly intense, fragrant flavor, these are the most widely used.

Noodles: Most types are interchangeable, but two, rice stick noodles and mung bean noodles, can be crisp-fried. Dried noodles are usually soaked in cold water for 10 to 20 minutes until softened, before cooking; in general, the weight will have doubled after soaking. After draining, the cooking will usually be brief.

Mung bean noodles: Also called glass, shining, bean thread or cellophane noodles, these noodles are tough and semi-transparent raw. Stir into soups or stir-fry with vegetables. Soak in warm water for 5 minutes for general use, but use unsoaked in deep-frying.

Dried Chinese spaghetti: This thin firm noodle cooks quickly. Any thin spaghetti-type noodle can be substituted. Chinese egg noodles are also sold fresh in supermarkets and Asian markets.

Fresh rice noodles: Packaged cooked and wet in wide, pliable 'hanks'. To use, without unwinding, cut into ribbons and stir into a dish just to warm through.

Rice stick noodles: Long, thin dried noodles made from rice flour, rice sticks (also known as rice vermicelli) can be fried directly in hot oils and increase many times in volume. A good accompaniment for any Chinese-style dish.

Soba: This spaghetti-size noodle, made from buckwheat flour, is often used in Japanese soups. Ideal for cold noodle salads and very quick cooking.

Oriental eggplant: These long, thin eggplants are tastier than the large ones, do not need peeling and do not absorb much oil. Sold in supermarkets and Asian markets.

Oyster sauce: A thick, brown, bottled sauce with a rich, subtle flavor, made from concentrated oysters and soy sauce. Often used in beef and vegetable stir-fry dishes.

Palm sugar: Brown sugar with a slight caramelized flavor, sold in cakes. If unavailable, substitute 1/2 white and 1/2 Demerara sugars.

Pandanus (screwpine): Both the leaves and the distilled essence of the flowers, called kewra water or essence, are used to give an exotic, musky, grassy flavor to Thai sweet dishes.

Pea eggplant: Very small eggplants about the size of a pea, and usually the same color, although they can be white, purple or yellow. The fresh, slightly bitter taste is used raw in hot sauces and cooked in curries.

Pickled and preserved vegetables: Various types of vegetables, preserved, or pickled, in salt, are availabe in cans and plastic pouches, but if a label simply specifies 'Preserved Vegetable', it will invariably mean mustard greens. 'Turnip' is not the Western variety, but a type of radish.

Plum sauce: A thick, sweet Cantonese condiment made from plums, apricots, garlic, chiles, sugar, vinegar and flavorings. Use as a dip or a base for barbecue sauces.

Rice: Thais mainly use a good quality variety of long-grain white rice called 'fragrant' rice. Ordinary long-grain white rice can be substituted. To cook, rinse the rice several times in cold running water. Put the rice into a heavy saucepan with 1-1/4 cups water, cover and bring quicky to a boil. Uncover and stir vigorously until the water has evaporated. Reduce the heat to very low, cover the pan tightly with foil, then cover. Steam for 20 minutes until the rice is tender, light, fluffy and every grain is separate.
'Sticky or 'glutinous' rice: An aptly named short, round grain variety. It can be formed into balls and eaten with fingers, or used for desserts.
Ground browned rice: Sometimes added to dishes to give extra texture. For this, dry-fry raw long-grain white rice until well-browned, then grind finely.

Rice vinegar: The mildest of all vinegars, with a sweet, delicate flavor and available in several varieties. If possible, use a pale rice vinegar for

Above: *Rice, Chicken and Mushrooms (page 77).*

light-colored sweet-and-sour dishes, and try a dark variety for dipping sauces. If neither is available, use cider vinegar. Use Japanese rice vinegar for salad dressings, sauces, and pickling; Chinese vinegar is not strong enough.

Rice wine: Made from fermented rice and yeast, this mellow wine is widely used for stir-fry cooking. Similar to sherry in color, bouquet and alcohol content (18%), but with its own distinctive flavor. If unavailable, substitute a good dry sherry.

Rose wine: Imparts an exotic quality to foods. Use sweet sherry as a substitute.

Sesame oil: Made from toasted sesame seeds, this has a rich, golden brown color and a nutty flavor and aroma. Has a low smoking point and can burn easily. As a seasoning, a teaspoon added to a stir-fry dish just before serving adds a delicious flavor.

Sesame seeds: Widely available, these add texture and flavor to stir-fry dishes. Dry-fry in the wok first to bring out flavor, then stir-fry and use as a garnish. Black sesame seeds can be interchanged with white ones – dry-fry them in the same way.

Shallots: Thai red shallots are smaller than Western ones. They have quite

a pronounced flavor that is almost fruity rather than pungent. Ordinary shallots can be substituted.

Shrimps, dried: Whole dried shrimps are used to add texture and flavor.

Shrimp paste: A pungent, salty paste that is packed in jars, cans and plastic packages. It should be kept refrigerated.

Soy sauces: This essential Chinese condiment, flavoring and dipping sauce is made from a fermented mixture of soybeans, flour and water. The more delicate light soy sauce is most common. It is salty, but can be diluted with water. Dark soy sauce is thicker and sweeter, containing molasses or caramel. Japanese soy sauce, shoyu, is always naturally fermented.

Spring roll skins: These paper-thin, wheat-flour dough skins are sometimes sold as lumpia skins. They are thinner and fry more crisply than thicker Cantonese egg roll skins. They can be refrozen.

Star anise: This eight-pointed star-shaped pod has a mild liqorice flavor and is used in marinades.

Star fruit: Star fruit, also known as carambola, are long, almost translucent yellow, ridged fruit. The whole

fruit is edible, and when cut across the width, the slices resemble five-pointed stars. Raw star fruit have a pleasant, citrus-like, juicy sharpness, but when poached the flavor is more distinctive.

Szechuan peppercorns: These aromatic, reddish brown dried berries have a mildly spicy flavor. Toast in a dry wok or skillet before grinding to a powder.

Tamarind: Sold in sticky brown-black blocks, tamarind provides a sharp, slightly fruity taste. To make tamarind water, break off a 1-ounce piece, pour over 1-1/4 cups boiling water. Break up the lump with a spoon, then leave for about 30 minutes, stirring occasionally. Strain off the tamarind water, pressing on the pulp. Discard the remaining debris and keep the water in a jar in the refrigerator for up to 5 days. Ready-to-use tamarind syrup can sometimes be bought; it is usually more concentrated, so less is required.

Thai basil: Also called 'holy basil', Thai basil leaves are darker and their flavor slightly deeper, less 'fresh', than ordinary sweet basil. Bundles of leaves can be frozen whole in a plastic bag for up to about 2 weeks; remove leaves as required and add straight to dishes. Substitute Thai sweet basil or ordinary sweet basil, if necessary.

Thai mint: This has a spearmint flavor. If unavailable, Western spearmint or garden mint are the best substitutes.

Water chestnuts: A starchy, bland, crunchy tuber. Use raw in salads, or add to soups and stir-fries. Widely sold in cans; rinse in cold water, or drop briefly into boiling water then rinse, to remove any metallic taste.

Won-ton skins: These smooth, wheat-flour-dough wrappers about 3 inches square are sold fresh and frozen in supermarkets and Asian markets.

Yellow bean paste/sauce: This thick, aromatic, spicy sauce is made from fermented yellow beans, flour and salt. It is used to flavor fish, poultry and vegetables.

Cooks in the Far East often spend more time in the kitchen preparing the ingredients than cooking them. Cooking utensils are few, practical and versatile, and are designed to make the most efficient and economical use of heat.

Cleaver: Cooks in the Far East use a cleaver for all tasks that require a knife, from carving delicate flower shapes from vegetables to chopping bones. A chef will select the cleaver that has the right size and weight for his or her physique. Frequent honing on a stone ensures that it is always razor-sharp.

Chopsticks: Special long chopsticks are used for cooking, particularly stir-frying. For eating, pick up a chopstick as you would a pen or pencil, square ends pointing upwards and rounded or tapered ends downwards, and let an equal amount of the chopstick protrude on each side of the hand. Now, instead of holding the chopstick with your thumb and index finger, as you would hold a pencil, hold it with the tips of the fourth and the little finger and let the upper part of the chopstick rest comfortably in the base of the thumb and the index finger. This is the stationary chopstick. With your other hand, pick up the second chopstick and place it directly above the first, and parallel to it. Hold the upper stick firmly with the thumb, index and middle fingers as you would a pencil. Use the thumb to brace the stationary chopstick securely against the tip of the fourth finger. There should be about 1 inch of space between the sticks. Press the upper chopstick down with the index and third finger so that it meets the stationary chopstick to pick up the food. Tap the ends of the chopsticks gently on the table to make sure they are even as they will not work efficiently unless aligned.

Pestle and mortar: Used during the preparation of the majority of savory dishes. A small food procesor or a coffee grinder kept specifically for the purpose will take away the effort but will not produce quite the same results. When used for fibrous ingredients such as galangal and lemon grass, the pestle and mortar crushes the fibers rather than cutting them

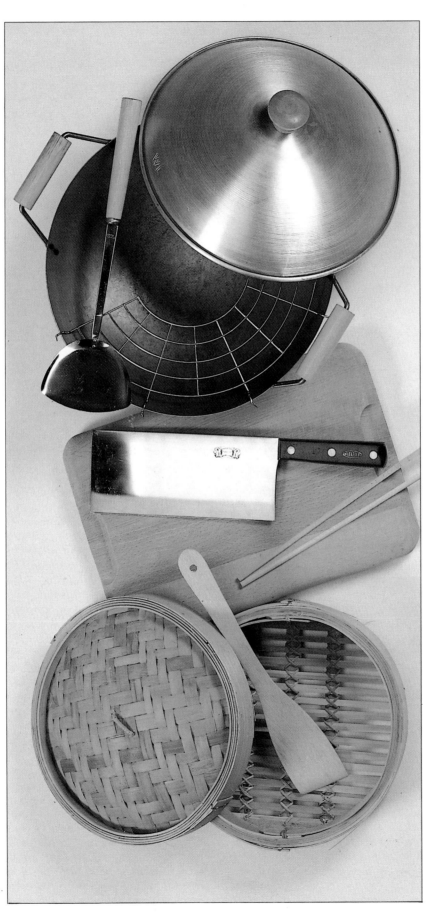

and so releases the flavor in juices and oils more successfully.

Rack: For using in a wok to support the steaming basket or container of food above the level of the water.

Skimmer: Shallow, wide, metal mesh skimmers are used for lifting deep-fried food from the oil, and for serving pieces of food from 'pot-style' meals.

Spatula: For efficiency, safety and comfort when stir-frying, a spatula with a curved blade that follows the contours of the wok, and a long handle that allows the hand to be kept away from the heat, is used.

Steamers: Bamboo steamers, designed to sit over a wok, are often stacked two or more high so that a number of dishes can be cooked at the same time. The steam is absorbed by the bamboo lid preventing water dripping on to the food. So that all the nourishing juices and flavor are retained, the food is often placed on a plate in the steamer and served directly from it.

Whisk: A whisk about 10 inches long and consisting of thin strips of bamboo tied together at the top is used for cleaning a wok.

Wire baskets: Bamboo-handled wire baskets are used to quickly and easily plunge noodles into boiling water for the requisite short cooking time before speedily lifting them out. A Far Eastern kitchen will usually have a set of baskets, as different ones are used for different types of noodles.

Wok: The wok is the cornerstone of Far Eastern cooking and is used for frying, stir-frying, deep-frying and steaming food. Woks come in many sizes; a useful size to buy is about 12 to 14 inches in diameter across the top. Choose one that has good deep sides and some weight. Carbon steel is preferable to light stainless steel or aluminum as these tend to develop hot spots which cause sticking, and do not withstand intense heat so well. Non-stick woks and electric ones do not reach sufficiently high temperatures. A metal ring or stand is often used to hold a round-bottomed wok steady over the heat.

CUTTING AND SLICING TECHNIQUES

Although stir-frying is quick and easy, preparation of ingredients is very important and every one must be prepared before cooking begins. Cutting and slicing Far-Eastern style is an art. The size and shape of ingredients determines cooking time, and there is little time for foods to absorb flavors and seasoning. Therefore, cut vegetables thinly, with as many cut surfaces as possible. Cut meats, fish and poultry generally across the grain, for maximum tenderness.

Slicing: Hold food firmly against a cutting board with one hand and, with a knife, slice the food straight down into thin strips. Hold a cleaver with your index finger extended over the top edge and your thumb on the near side, to guide the cutting edge. Hold the food with the other hand, tucking your fingers under, so the blade rests against your knuckles for safety. For matchstick-thin strips, square off the sides of the prepared vegetable, cut crossways into 2-inch lengths. Stack a few slices and cut even lengthwise strips.

Shredding: Foods such as cabbage or spinach are easily shredded by piling up a few leaves and cutting lengthwise into thin fine shreds. Roll large leaves, jelly-roll style, before cutting, to reduce width. Meat and poultry breasts or cutlets are easier to shred if frozen for about 20 minutes.

Horizontal slicing: To cut thick foods into two or more thin pieces to be sliced or shredded, hold the cleaver or knife parallel to the cutting board. Place one hand flat on the food surface and press down while slicing horizontally into the food. Repeat if necessary.

Diagonal slicing: Most 'long' vegetables, such as green onions, asparagus or zucchini look attractive and more surface area is exposed for quicker cooking if sliced on the diagonal. Angle the cleaver or knife and cut.

Roll cutting: This is like diagonal cutting, but is suitable for larger or tougher, long vegetables, such as celery or large carrots. Make a diagonal slice at one end, then turn the

vegetable 180 degrees and make another diagonal slice. Continue until the whole vegetable is cut into triangular pieces about 1 inch long.

Dicing: Cut food into slices, then into lengthwise sticks. Stack the sticks and cut crosswise into even-sized cubes.

Chopping: First cut the food into long strips, stack them and, holding them with one hand, fingers tucked under, cut crosswise with a knife or cleaver. Use a rocking motion, keeping the tip of the knife or cleaver against the board and using the knuckles as a guide.

SEASONING AND CLEANING THE WOK

Authentic carbon steel woks must be scrubbed to remove the protective coating of machine oil applied during manufacturing and seasoned before use. To remove this sometimes thick, sticky oil, scrub the wok vigorously with kitchen detergent and hot water. This is the only time you should scrub the wok, unless it rusts during storage. Dry the wok and place it over low heat for a few minutes to dry thoroughly.

To season, add 2 tablespoons vegetable oil and, using a double thickness of folded paper towels, rub a thin film of oil all over the inside of the wok. Heat the wok for a few more minutes and wipe again. The paper will probably be black from machine oil residue. Repeat until the paper stays clean. The wok is now ready for use.

Food rarely sticks to a seasoned wok, so an ordinary wash in hot water with no detergent should suffice. If any food has stuck, use a bamboo wok brush, or ordinary plastic kitchen scrubber. Dry the wok thoroughly and place it over a low heat to prevent rust during storage. As a precaution, rub the inside surface of the dry wok with 1 teaspoon of oil. If the wok rusts, repeat the seasoning process.

COOKING TECHNIQUES

Stir-frying: Probably the most important technique in stir-frying is preheating the wok. This prevents food sticking and absorbing excess oil. Place the wok over medium heat and wait a few minutes until the wok is very hot, then add the oil and swirl to quickly coat the bottom and sides of the wok with oil.

For recipes that begin by adding the flavoring ingredients, such as garlic, gingerroot and green onions, to the oil, it should be only moderately hot or these delicate ingredients may burn or become bitter. If, however, the first ingredient added is a meat or hearty vegetable, make the oil very hot, just below smoking point. As other ingredients are added, stir-fry over high heat by stirring and tossing them with the metal spatula or spoon. Allow meat to rest a minute on one side before stirring, to cook and brown. Keep the food moving from the center, up and out onto the side. If a sauce to be thickened with cornstarch is added to the dish, remove the wok briefly from the heat and push the food away from the center so the sauce-thickening mixture goes directly to the bottom of the wok; stir vigorously and then continue tossing the ingredients in the boiling sauce to coat the food evenly.

Deep-frying: Deep-frying in a wok uses less oil. Foods are often marinated first in soy sauce and spices, then sometimes coated in batter; a mixture of cornstarch and egg white is the most usual in Chinese cuisine. Often, food is fried until almost cooked, then removed from the oil. The oil is reheated and the food added again to finish cooking and become really crisp.

Steaming: Steaming is far more popular in the Far East than in the West and is used to cook meat, poultry, fish, dim sum, other pastries and desserts. It was developed as a fuel-saving measure as several foods can be cooked at once in baskets, which are often made of bamboo, stacked above each other. Foods that require the most cooking are put to cook first, and those needing less time are placed on top in succession, as the cooking proceeds.

Red cooking: Food, usually in large pieces, is cooked slowly in dark soy sauce, sometimes with other flavorings added. During the lengthy cooking, which may be as long as 4 hours, the soy imparts a fairly dark, reddish brown color and a rich flavor to the food. Because of the large amount of soy sauce that is used, the food can also be salty, so sugar may be added to counteract it.

GREEN ONION BRUSHES

CHILE FLOWERS

4 green onions

Trim away some of green tops of each green onion. Cut off each white bulb where it starts to turn green.

Using a small pair of kitchen scissors, make a cut from dark green end of a leaf to about halfway along the length. Continue to cut leaf into thin strips. Repeat with remaining leaves.

Place green onion into a bowl of chilled water. Let stand a few seconds for strips to curl; check by lifting from water several times that they do not curl too tightly. Repeat with remaining green onions. Place on paper towels to dry before using.

Makes 4.

4 small chiles

Cut off tip of 1 chile. Insert scissors in hole and cut through chile flesh almost to stem end. Give chile a quarter turn, make another similar cut, then repeat twice more.

Remove and discard seeds. Cut through each quarter once or twice more to make thin petals.

Place chile in a bowl of chilled water. Let stand 5 to 10 minutes for petals to open into a flower shape. Repeat with remaining chiles. Place on paper towels to dry before using.

Makes 4.

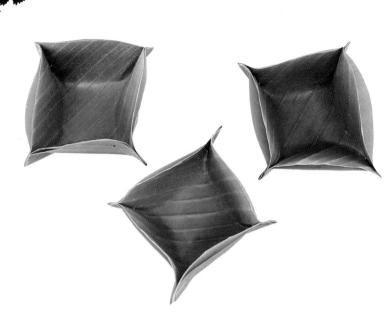

BANANA LEAF CUPS

CARROT FLOWERS

8 pieces banana leaf, each about 5 inches square

Place two pieces of banana leaf with dull sides facing each other. Invert a bowl measuring 4 inches in diameter on top of leaves. Cut around bowl.

1 young tender carrot, peeled

Hold carrot pointed end down. Using a small, sharp knife, make a cut toward the point to form a petal-shape. Take care not to slice all the way through. Repeat cuts around carrot to make a 4-petalled flower.

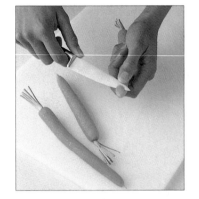

Form a 2-inch pleat about 1-1/2 inches deep in the edge of banana leaf circle. Staple together.

Angle knife slightly, then apply light pressure to separate carrot flower from carrot. For first few flowers, it may be necessary to ease every petal in this way, but with a little practice, flowers will come away easily with a twist of the knife.

Make an identical pleat in the opposite side of the circle, then repeat twice more at points equidistant among the two pleats, to make a slightly opened, squared-off cup. Repeat with remaining pieces of banana leaf.

Makes 4 cups.

Repeat along length of carrot. Arrange flowers individually or group them into clusters.

Note: To improve color, drop flowers in boiling water 1 minute, then drain and rinse under cold running water. Dry well.

PASTES, SAUCES & DIPS

GREEN CURRY PASTE

2 teaspoons coriander seeds
1 teaspoon cumin seeds
1 teaspoon peppercorns
8 fresh green chiles, seeded, chopped
3 shallots, chopped
4 garlic cloves, crushed
3 cilantro roots, chopped
1-inch piece galangal, chopped
2 stalks lemon grass, chopped
2 kaffir lime leaves, chopped
2 teaspoons shrimp paste
2 tablespoons chopped cilantro leaves

Heat a wok, add coriander seeds and cumin seeds and heat until aroma changes.

Using a pestle and mortar or small food processor, crush coriander seeds and cumin seeds with peppercorns.

Add remaining ingredients and pound or mix to a smooth paste. Store in an airtight jar in refrigerator for up to four weeks.

Makes about 1/2 cup.

Note: The yield and hotness will vary according to the size and heat of the chiles.

RED CURRY PASTE

1 tablespoon coriander seeds
1 teaspoon cumin seeds
1 teaspoon peppercorns
4 garlic cloves, chopped
3 cilantro roots, chopped
8 dried red chiles, seeded, chopped
2 stalks lemon grass, chopped
Grated peel of 1/2 lime
1-1/4-inch piece galangal, chopped
2 teaspoons shrimp paste

Heat a wok, add coriander seeds and cumin seeds and heat until aroma changes. Using a pestle and mortar or small food processor, crush coriander and cumin seeds with peppercorns.

Add remaining ingredients and pound or mix to a smooth paste. Store in an airtight jar in refrigerator for up to 4 weeks.

Makes about 1/4 cup.

Note: The yield and hotness will vary according to the size and heat of the chiles.

FRAGRANT CURRY PASTE

NAM PRIK

2 garlic cloves, chopped
1 shallot, chopped
4 dried red chiles, seeded, chopped
1 thick stalk lemon grass, chopped
3 cilantro roots, chopped
Finely grated peel of 2 limes
1 kaffir lime leaf, torn
4 black peppercorns
1/2 teaspoon shrimp paste

1 tablespoon fish sauce
About 22 whole dried shrimp, chopped
3 garlic cloves, chopped
4 dried red chiles with seeds, chopped
2 tablespoons lime juice
1 fresh red or green chile, seeded, chopped
About 1 tablespoon pea eggplant, if desired, chopped

Using a pestle and mortar or a small food processor, pound or mix together fish sauce, shrimp, garlic, dried chiles and lime juice to a paste.

Using a pestle and mortar or small food processor, pound or mix together garlic, shallot, chiles, lemon grass and cilantro roots.

Stir in fresh chile and eggplant, if using. Transfer to a small serving bowl.

Add lime peel, lime leaf, peppercorns and shrimp paste, and pound or mix to a smooth paste. Store in an airtight jar in the refrigerator for up to four weeks.

Makes about 6 tablespoons.

Serve with a selection of raw vegetables. Store in an airtight jar in refrigerator several weeks.

Makes 6 to 8 servings.

DIPPING SAUCE 1

6 tablespoons lime juice
1-1/2 to 2 teaspoons crushed palm sugar
1/2 teaspoon fish sauce
1/2 teaspoon very finely chopped shallot
1/2 teaspoon very finely chopped fresh green chile
1/2 teaspoon finely chopped fresh red chile

DIPPING SAUCE 2

1/2 cup tamarind water, see page 11
1/2 to 3/4 teaspoon crushed palm sugar
1 or 2 drops fish sauce
1/2 teaspoon very finely chopped green onion
1/2 teaspoon very finely chopped garlic
1/2 teaspoon finely chopped fresh red chile

In a small bowl, stir together lime juice and sugar until sugar has dissolved. Adjust amount of sugar, if desired.

In a small saucepan, gently heat tamarind water and sugar until sugar has dissolved.

Stir in fish sauce, shallot and chile. Pour into a small serving bowl. Serve with deep-fried fish, fish fritters, won tons or spring rolls.

Makes 4 servings.

Remove pan from heat. Add fish sauce, stir in green onion, garlic and chile. Pour into a small serving bowl and cool.

Makes 4 servings.

SOUPS

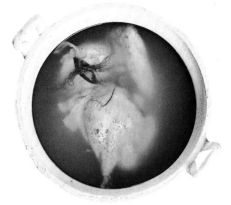

CHINESE CHICKEN STOCK

½ stewing chicken
1 ham hock, split
4 slices gingerroot
4 green onions, chopped
1 tablespoon chopped parsley
2 quarts water

Place all ingredients in a large saucepan and bring to a boil. Skim. Reduce heat so liquid simmers, cover gently and cook 3 hours.

Pour into a sieve lined with cheesecloth, placed over a large bowl. Cool completely in a bowl of iced water or refrigerator. Store, covered, in the refrigerator, or freeze in convenient quantities.

Makes 7 cups.

Note: Chinese cooks use Chicken Stock for fish dishes (they do not make fish stock). If fish stock is preferred, substitute a favorite recipe.

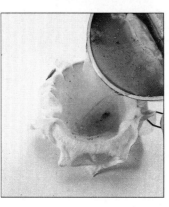

MUSHROOM SOUP

24 dried black winter mushrooms, soaked in hot water 25 minutes, drained
1/2-inch piece gingerroot, peeled and cut into 6 slices
2 green onions, finely chopped
1-1/2 teaspoons sea salt
6 cups Chinese Chicken Stock
2 teaspoons rice wine or dry sherry
1 teaspoon brown sugar
Parsley to garnish

Trim mushrooms and place in a small saucepan with half the gingerroot and half the green onions. Add 1/2 teaspoon salt and cover with cold water. Bring slowly to a boil, then simmer 3 minutes.

Drain. Pour stock into a medium saucepan, add mushroom mixture and remaining ingredients. Bring slowly to a boil, reduce heat, cover, and simmer gently 30 to 35 minutes. Serve hot garnished with parsley.

Makes 4 servings.

HOT AND SOUR SOUP

4 dried black winter mushrooms, soaked in hot water
    for 25 minutes
1/4 (14-oz.) can Szechuan preserved vegetables, finely
    sliced
1/4 (14-oz.) can Chinese pickled green vegetables,
    finely sliced
3 green onions, finely chopped
3 slices gingerroot
3-1/4 cups water
1-1/2 teaspoons rice wine or dry sherry
1 tablespoon light soy sauce
2 tofu cakes, finely sliced (8 ounces)
1 teaspoon cornstarch dissolved in 2 teaspoons water
1 teaspoon sesame oil

Drain mushrooms, discard stalks, squeeze out all the liquid, then slice very finely. In a medium saucepan, bring all the ingredients except cornstarch mixture and sesame oil to a boil; cook for 3 minutes.

Stir in cornstarch mixture, simmer, still stir-ring, until thickened, then add sesame oil.

Makes 4 servings.

LEMON GRASS SOUP

6 to 8 ounces raw shrimp
2 teaspoons vegetable oil
2-1/2 cups light fish stock
2 thick stalks lemon grass, finely chopped
3 tablespoons lime juice
1 tablespoon fish sauce
3 kaffir lime leaves, chopped
1/2 fresh red chile, thinly sliced
1/2 fresh green chile, thinly sliced
1/2 teaspoon crushed palm sugar
Cilantro leaves to garnish

Peel shrimp and remove dark veins running down their backs; reserve shrimp and shells.

In a wok, heat oil, add shrimp shells and fry, stirring occasionally, until they change color. Stir in stock, bring to a boil, reduce heat and simmer 20 minutes. Strain stock and return to wok; discard shells. Add lemon grass, lime juice, fish sauce, lime leaves, chiles and sugar. Simmer 2 minutes.

Add shrimp and cook just below simmering 2 to 3 minutes until shrimp are pink. Serve in heated bowls garnished with cilantro.

Makes 4 servings.

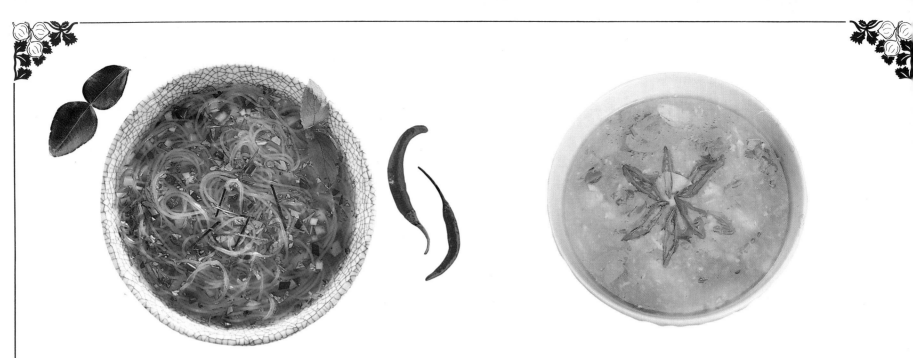

VERMICELLI SOUP

5 cups chicken stock
1 small onion, chopped
2 stalks lemon grass, chopped, crushed
2 kaffir lime leaves, shredded
1 tablespoon lime juice
3 garlic cloves, chopped
2 fresh red chiles, seeded, chopped
1-1/2-inch piece galangal, chopped
1-1/2 tablespoons fish sauce
2 teaspoons crushed palm sugar
4 ounces clear vermicelli, soaked in cold water
    10 minutes, drained
2 tablespoons coarsely chopped cilantro
Thai basil leaves to garnish

Put stock, onion, lemon grass, lime leaves, lime juice, garlic, chiles and galangal into a saucepan and simmer 20 minutes.

Stir in fish sauce and sugar. When sugar has dissolved, add vermicelli and cook 1 minute. Stir in cilantro. Spoon into warmed bowls and garnish with basil leaves.

Makes 4 to 6 servings.

CHICKEN & ASPARAGUS SOUP

2 cups Chinese Chicken Stock, see page 22
1-1/2 cups finely sliced cooked chicken breast
2 teaspoons cornstarch dissolved in 1 tablespoon water
12 button mushrooms, sliced
1/4 (14-oz.) can asparagus tips, drained and chopped
1/4 (14-oz.) can sweetcorn, drained
1-1/2 teaspoons sea salt
1 teaspoon sesame oil to serve
2 green onions, finely chopped to garnish

In a saucepan bring chicken stock to the boil. Add the chicken, simmer 2 to 3 minutes, then stir in cornstarch mixture and simmer, still stirring, until thickened.

Reduce heat, add mushrooms, asparagus and sweetcorn and heat through gently but thoroughly. Season with salt. Serve sprinkled with sesame oil and garnished with chopped green onions.

Makes 4 servings.

MEATBALL SOUP

CHICKEN & MUSHROOM SOUP

1 pound pork tenderloin, finely ground
3 dried black winter mushrooms, soaked in hot water
    25 minutes, drained and finely chopped
2 green onions, very finely chopped
2 tablespoons light soy sauce
Sea salt
2/3 cup cornstarch for coating
1/2 teaspoon ground black pepper
3 tablespoons peanut oil
7 cups Chinese Chicken Stock, see page 22, plus 1 cup
    water
Chopped parsley to garnish

2 garlic cloves, crushed
4 cilantro sprigs
1-1/2 teaspoons peppercorns, crushed
1 tablespoon vegetable oil
4-1/2 cups chicken stock
5 pieces dried Chinese black mushrooms, soaked in
    cold water 30 minutes, drained, coarsely chopped
1 tablespoon fish sauce
4 ounces chicken, cut into strips
2 green onions, thinly sliced
Cilantro sprigs to garnish

In a bowl, mix together pork, mushrooms, green onions, soy sauce and 1 teaspoon salt. Pass through the finest blade of a grinder. Roll mixture into 1-inch balls. Roll balls in cornstarch to lightly coat.

Using a pestle and mortar or a small food processor, pound or mix garlic, 4 cilantro sprigs and peppercorns to a paste. In a wok, heat vegetable oil, add paste and cook, stirring, 1 minute. Stir in stock, mushrooms and fish sauce. Simmer 5 minutes.

In a wok, heat oil and fry the balls about 4 minutes until lightly and evenly browned. Drain on paper towels. In a saucepan, heat chicken stock and water to a boil. Reduce heat so stock simmers, then add meatballs. Season with salt and pepper. Garnish with chopped parsley.

Makes 4 servings.

Add chicken, reduce heat so liquid simmers and cook gently 5 minutes. Scatter green onions over surface and garnish with cilantro sprigs.

Makes 4 servings.

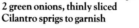

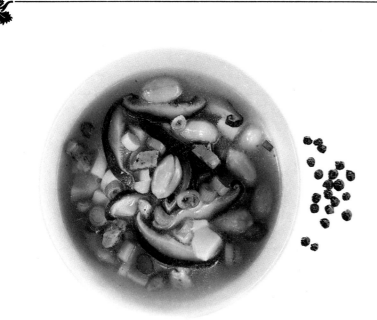

—PORK & PEANUT SOUP—

4 cilantro roots, chopped
2 garlic cloves, chopped
1 teaspoon peppercorns, cracked
1 tablespoon vegetable oil
8 ounces lean pork, very finely chopped
4 green onions, chopped
3 cups veal stock
2 ounces raw shelled peanuts
6 pieces dried black Chinese mushrooms, soaked 20
    minutes, drained and chopped
4 ounces bamboo shoots, coarsely chopped
1 tablespoon fish sauce

Using a pestle and mortar, pound to a paste
cilantro roots, garlic and peppercorns.

In a wok, heat oil, add peppercorn paste and
cook 2 to 3 minutes, stirring occasionally.
Add pork and green onions and stir 1-1/2
minutes.

Stir stock, peanuts and mushrooms into wok,
then cook at just below boiling 7 minutes.
Add bamboo shoots and fish sauce and
continue to cook 3 to 4 minutes.

Makes 3 to 4 servings.

—CHICKEN & COCONUT SOUP—

3-3/4 cups coconut milk
4 ounces boneless skinless chicken breast, cut into
    strips
2 stalks lemon grass, bruised and thickly sliced
2 green onions, thinly sliced
3 or 4 fresh red chiles, seeded, sliced
Juice of 1-1/2 limes
1 tablespoon fish sauce
1 tablespoon cilantro leaves, shredded
Cilantro leaves to garnish

Bring coconut milk to just below boiling.
Add chicken and lemon grass.

Adjust heat so liquid simmers, then poach
chicken, uncovered, until tender, about 4
minutes.

Add green onions and chiles. Heat briefly,
then remove from heat and stir in lime juice,
fish sauce and shredded cilantro. Garnish
with cilantro leaves.

Makes 4 servings.

APPETIZERS

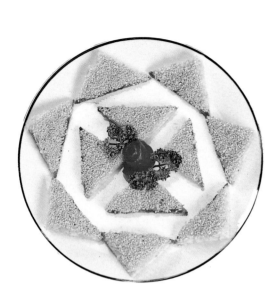

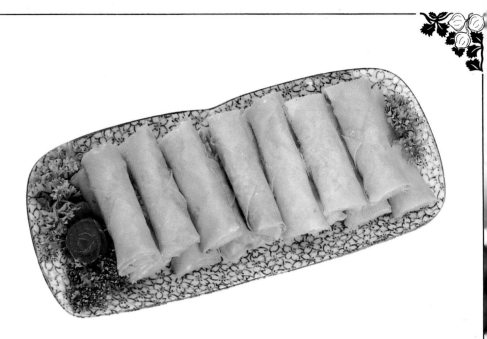

SHRIMP TOASTS

2 tablespoons pork fat, finely ground
6 ounces peeled uncooked shrimp, finely ground
1/4 teaspoon sea salt
1 tablespoon cornstarch
1 egg white, lightly beaten
White pepper
3 thin white bread slices, crusts removed
2/3 cup sesame seeds
2-1/2 cups vegetable oil

In a bowl, mix together fat, shrimps, salt, cornstarch and egg white. Season with white pepper.

Spread shrimp mixture on one side of each bread slice.

Coat with a thick layer of sesame seeds, and press well into the spread. Cut each slice into 4 triangles. In a wok, heat oil until smoking, reduce heat slightly, then carefully add the triangles, coated-side down. Deep-fry 2 to 3 minutes until golden brown. Drain on paper towels. Serve hot.

Makes 4 servings.

SPRING ROLLS

20 spring roll skins
4 cups vegetable oil
FILLING:
3 tablespoons peanut oil
50 mung bean sprouts
6 green onions, thinly shredded
1 cup julienned carrots
2 cups thinly sliced button mushrooms
1 garlic clove, very finely chopped
1/4 teaspoon five-spice powder
1 tablespoon light soy sauce
1 teaspoon sea salt

To make the filling, heat peanut oil in a wok and stir-fry vegetables, garlic and tofu about 1 minute. Add five-spice powder, soy sauce and salt and continue stir-frying 2 minutes. Cool. To fill the skins, lay one flat on a work surface. Place a portion of filling slightly off-center. Fold the sides of the skin neatly over the filling, then roll up to enclose the filling completely. Brush around the edges with beaten egg to seal.

In a wok or fryer, heat vegetable oil until smoking. Reduce heat slightly, add 4 spring rolls and fry 4 minutes, until crisp and golden. Drain on paper towels. Keep warm. Re-heat oil, reduce heat and cook 4 more spring rolls. Repeat with remaining rolls.

Variations: Substitute 1 cup chopped, prepared shrimp, see page 19, in place of the tofu.

Makes 4 servings.

─ PORK DIM SUM ─

3/4 pound ground pork
1/4 pound raw shelled shrimp, ground
1-1/2 tablespoons soy sauce
1/2 tablespoon rice wine or dry sherry
1/2 tablespoon sesame oil
1/2 tablespoon sugar
Dash of pepper
1 egg white
1-1/2 tablespoons cornstarch
30 won-ton skins
Fresh or frozen green peas or chopped hard-cooked egg
    yolks, for garnish

To make filling: Mix together ground pork, ground shrimp, soy sauce, rice wine or dry sherry, sesame oil, sugar, pepper and egg white until mixture is well blended and smooth. Stir in cornstarch. Divide into 30 portions. Cut off the edges of won-ton skins to form circles, if necessary. Place 1 portion of filling in the middle of a won-ton skin. Gather the edges of the won-ton skin around the meat filling. Dip a teaspoon in water and use to smooth the surface of the meat.

Garnish by placing a green pea or chopped egg yolk on top of meat. Gather the edges to form a waist. Repeat with remaining won-ton skins and meat filling. Line a steamer with a damp cloth; steam over high heat 5 minutes. Remove and serve.

Makes 30 dumplings.

─ SHRIMP DIM SUM ─

3/4 pound raw shelled shrimp, ground
1 (4-oz.) can bamboo shoots, chopped
4 tablespoons water
1-1/2 tablespoons soy sauce
1/2 tablespoon rice wine or dry sherry
1/2 teaspoon sugar
1/2 teaspoon sesame oil
Dash of pepper
1-1/2 tablespoons cornstarch
DOUGH:
2-1/2 cups all-purpose flour
2/3 cup boiling water
1/3 cup cold water
1 tablespoon vegetable oil

To make filling: Mix together all ingredients except cornstarch until the mixture is well blended and smooth. Stir in cornstarch. Divide into 30 portions.

To make dough: Put 2 cups of flour in a medium size bowl. Reserve remainder and use for hands if they become sticky. Stir in boiling water. Add cold water and oil. Mix to form dough; knead until smooth. Roll dough into a long, rope shape and cut it into 30 pieces. Use a rolling pin to roll each portion into a thin 2-inch circle.

Place 1 portion of the filling in the middle of a dough circle. Bring the opposite edges together and pinch them together to hold. Repeat with remaining circles and filling. Line a steamer with a damp cloth. Set the dumplings about 1 inch apart. Steam over high heat 5 minutes. Remove and serve.

Makes 30 dumplings.

GOLD BAGS

4 ounces peeled cooked shrimp, finely chopped
2 ounces canned water chestnuts, finely chopped
2 green onions, white part only, finely chopped
1 teaspoon fish sauce
Freshly ground pepper
16 won-ton skins
Vegetable oil for deep-frying
Dipping Sauce 2, see page 20
Cilantro sprig to garnish

In a small bowl, mix together shrimp, water chestnuts, green onions, fish sauce and pepper.

To shape each bag, put a small amount of shrimp mixture in center of each won-ton skin. Dampen edges of skins with a little water, then bring up over filling to form a bag. Press edges together to seal.

In a wok, heat oil to 375F (190C). Add bags in batches and fry about 2 to 3 minutes until crisp and golden. Using a slotted spoon, transfer to paper towels to drain. Serve hot with Dipping Sauce. Garnish with cilantro sprig.

Makes 16.

CORN CAKES

2 cups canned or cooked whole-kernel corn, drained
1 tablespoon Green Curry Paste, see page 18
2 tablespoons all-purpose flour
3 tablespoons rice flour
3 green onions, finely chopped
1 egg, beaten
2 teaspoons fish sauce
Vegetable oil for deep-frying
1-inch piece cucumber
Dipping Sauce 1, see page 20
1 tablespoon ground roasted peanuts

Place corn in a blender, add curry paste, all-purpose flour, rice flour, green onions, egg and fish sauce and mix together until corn is slightly chopped. Form into about 16 cakes. Heat oil in a wok to 350F (175C), then deep-fry one batch of corn cakes about 3 minutes until golden-brown.

Using a slotted spoon, transfer cakes to paper towels to drain. Keep warm in a warm oven while frying remaining cakes. Peel cucumber, quarter lengthwise, remove seeds and slice thinly. Place in a small bowl and mix in dipping sauce and ground peanuts. Serve with warm corn cakes.

Makes about 16.

EGG NESTS

1 tablespoon chopped cilantro roots
1 garlic clove, chopped
1/2 teaspoon peppercorns, cracked
1 tablespoon peanut oil
1/2 small onion, finely chopped
4 ounces lean pork, very finely chopped
4 ounces peeled raw shrimp, chopped
2 teaspoons fish sauce
3 tablespoons vegetable oil
2 eggs
3 fresh red chiles, seeded, cut into thin strips
20 to 30 cilantro leaves
Cilantro sprigs to garnish

Add vegetable oil to wok and place over medium heat. In a small bowl, beat eggs. Spoon a small amount of beaten egg into a cone of waxed paper with a very small hole in the pointed end. Hold almost directly over wok, move above surface of wok, so trail of egg flows onto it and sets in threads. Quickly repeat, moving in another direction directly over threads. Repeat until there are 4 criss-crossed layers of egg.

Using a pestle and mortar, pound together cilantro roots, garlic and peppercorns. In a wok, heat peanut oil, add peppercorn mixture and onion and stir-fry 1 minute.

Using a spatula, transfer nest to paper towels. Repeat with remaining eggs to make nests. Place nests with flat-side facing down. Place 2 chile strips to form a cross on each nest.

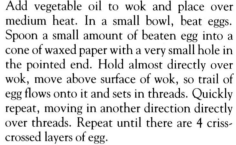

Add pork, stir-fry 1 minute, then add shrimp. Stir-fry 45 seconds. Quickly stir in fish sauce, then transfer mixture to a bowl. Using paper towels, wipe out wok.

Top with cilantro leaves, then about 1 table-spoon of pork mixture. Fold nests over filling, turn over and arrange on serving plate. Garnish with cilantro sprigs.

Makes 4 servings.

STEAMED CRAB

1 garlic clove, chopped
1 small shallot, chopped
Stems from 6 cilantro sprigs, finely chopped
6 ounces cooked crabmeat
4 ounces lean pork, very finely chopped, cooked
1 egg, beaten
1 tablespoon coconut cream, see page 10
2 teaspoons fish sauce
Freshly ground pepper
Cilantro leaves, to garnish
1 red chile, seeded, cut into thin strips

Using a pestle and mortar, pound to a paste garlic, shallot and cilantro stems. In a bowl, stir together garlic paste, crabmeat, pork, egg, coconut cream, fish sauce and plenty of pepper until evenly mixed.

Divide among dishes, arrange cilantro leaves and chile strips on tops. Place steaming basket over a saucepan of boiling water and steam about 12 minutes until mixture is firm.

Makes 4 servings.

Note: Cleaned crab shells may be used instead of dishes for cooking.

STUFFED OMELET

2 tablespoons vegetable oil
1 small onion, quartered, thinly sliced
3 garlic cloves, chopped
8 cilantro roots, chopped
14 peppercorns, cracked
5 ounces lean pork, very finely chopped
5 ounces long beans or green beans, thinly sliced, cut into 1-1/4-inch lengths
8 eggs, beaten
2 teaspoons fish sauce
1/4 cup chopped cilantro
Cilantro sprigs to garnish

Heat 1-1/2 tablespoons of the oil in a wok, add onion and cook, stirring occasionally, until lightly browned.

Using a pestle and mortar or small food processor, pound or mix together garlic, cilantro roots and peppercorns. Stir into wok and cook, stirring occasionally, 2 minutes. Add pork, stir-fry 2 minutes, then stir in beans. Stir-fry 2 minutes. Cover wok and set aside.

In a small bowl, mix eggs with fish sauce and chopped cilantro. In a skillet, heat remaining oil, pour in half of egg mixture and tilt pan to form a thin, even layer. Cook just until set. Spoon half of pork filling down center. Fold sides over filling to form a square package, then slide onto a warmed plate. Keep warm and repeat with remaining mixtures. Garnish with cilantro sprigs.

Makes 4 to 6 servings.

STUFFED CHICKEN WINGS

4 large chicken wings
Small amount lean, ground pork
1/4 cup cooked peeled shrimp, chopped
3 green onions, finely chopped
2 large garlic cloves, chopped
3 cilantro roots, chopped
2 tablespoons fish sauce
Freshly ground black pepper
Vegetable oil for deep-frying
Rice flour for coating
Dipping Sauce 1, see page 20, to serve
Lettuce leaves, to garnish

Chop chicken flesh from wings. Make up to 6 ounces (about 1 cup) with pork, if necessary. Place chicken and pork, if used, in a bowl and thoroughly mix together with shrimp and green onions. Stuff mixture into chicken wings; set aside.

Bend wing joints backwards against joint. Using a small sharp knife or kitchen scissors, cut around top of bone that attaches wing to chicken body. Using blade of knife, scrape bone, turning back skin over unboned portion. Break bone free at joint.

Using a pestle and mortar, pound together garlic and cilantro roots. Stir in fish sauce and plenty of pepper. Pour over chicken wings, stirring them to coat with mixture, then set aside 30 minutes.

Ease skin over joint and detach from flesh and bone. Working down the next bones, scrape off flesh and skin taking care not to puncture skin. Break bones free at joint, leaving end section.

Heat oil in a wok to 350F (175C). Remove chicken wings from bowl, then toss in rice flour to coat completely. Add 2 at a time to oil and deep-fry 3 to 4 minutes until browned. Using a slotted spoon, transfer to paper towels to drain. Keep warm while frying remaining 2 chicken wings. Serve with sauce and garnish with lettuce leaves.

Makes 4 servings.

PORK TOASTS

6 ounces ground lean pork
1/4 cup finely chopped shrimp (2 ounces)
2 garlic cloves, chopped
1 tablespoon chopped cilantro
1-1/2 green onions, finely chopped
2 eggs, beaten
2 teaspoons fish sauce
Freshly ground pepper
4 day-old bread slices
1 tablespoon coconut milk
Vegetable oil for deep-frying
Cilantro leaves, thin red chile rings and cucumber
    slices to garnish

In a bowl, using a fork, mix together pork and shrimp, then thoroughly mix in garlic, cilantro, green onions, 1/4 of beaten eggs, the fish sauce and pepper. Divide mixture among bread slices, spreading it firmly to the edges. In a small bowl, stir together remaining eggs and coconut milk and brush over pork mixture. Trim crusts from bread, then cut each slice into rectangles.

Heat oil in a wok to 375F (190C). Add several rectangles at a time, pork-side down, and fry 3 to 4 minutes until crisp, turning over after 2 minutes. Using a slotted spoon, transfer to paper towels to drain, then keep warm in a warm oven. Check temperature of oil after frying each batch. Serve warm garnished with cilantro leaves, chile rings and cucumber slices.

Makes 4 to 6 servings.

PORK & NOODLE BALLS

3 garlic cloves, chopped
4 cilantro roots, chopped
1 cup ground lean pork (6 ounces)
1 small egg, beaten
2 teaspoons fish sauce
Freshly ground pepper
About 2 ounces egg thread noodles (1 coil)
Vegetable oil for deep-frying
Dipping Sauce 2, see page 20, to serve

Using a pestle and mortar or small food processor, pound or mix together garlic and cilantro roots. In a bowl, mix together pork, egg, fish sauce and pepper, then stir in garlic mixture.

Place noodles in a heatproof strainer and dip in boiling water 5 seconds if fresh, or about 2 minutes if dried, until separated. Remove and rinse immediately under cold running water. Form pork mixture into about 12 balls. Neatly and evenly wind 3 or 4 strands of noodles around each ball to cover completely.

Heat oil in a wok to 350F (175C). Using a slotted spoon, lower 4 to 6 balls into oil and cook about 3 minutes until golden-brown and pork is cooked through. Using a slotted spoon, transfer to paper towels to drain. Keep warm while cooking remaining balls. Serve hot with Dipping Sauce.

Makes about 12 balls.

FISH & SHELLFISH

SHRIMP WITH GARLIC

2 tablespoons vegetable oil
5 garlic cloves, chopped
1/4-inch slice gingerroot, very finely chopped
14 to 16 large shrimp, peeled, tails on, deveined
2 teaspoons fish sauce
2 tablespoons chopped cilantro
1 to 2 tablespoons water
Freshly ground pepper
Lettuce leaves, lime wedges and diced cucumber to
  serve

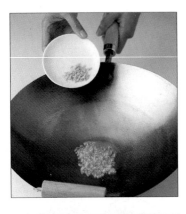

In a wok, heat oil, add garlic and fry until
browned.

Stir in gingerroot, heat 30 seconds, then add
shrimp and stir-fry 2 to 3 minutes until
beginning to turn pink. Stir in fish sauce,
cilantro, water and plenty of pepper. Boil 1 to
2 minutes.

Line a plate with lettuce; top with shrimp.
Serve with lime wedges and diced cucumber.

Makes 4 servings.

DEEP-FRIED COCONUT SHRIMP

1-1/2-inch piece cucumber
Dipping Sauce 2, see page 20
Leaves from 1 cilantro sprig, chopped
8 uncooked jumbo shrimp
Vegetable oil for deep-frying
BATTER:
4 ounces rice flour
3 tablespoons unsweetened shredded coconut
1 egg, separated
3/4 cup coconut milk
1 teaspoon fish sauce

Cut cucumber into quarters lengthwise,
remove and discard seeds, then thickly slice.
Place in a small bowl and add Dipping Sauce.
Stir in cilantro; set aside. Peel shrimp,
leaving tails on. Cut along back of each one
and remove black vein. Set shrimp aside.
Preheat oil in a wok to 350F (175C).

For batter, in a small bowl, stir together flour
and coconut. Gradually stir in egg yolk, coconut milk and fish sauce. In another small
bowl, beat egg white until stiff but not dry;
fold into batter. Dip shrimp in batter; add to
hot oil in batches. Cook 2 to 3 minutes until
golden. Using a slotted spoon, transfer to
paper towels to drain. Keep warm while
frying remaining shrimp. Serve shrimp with
sauce.

Makes 3 to 4 servings.

— STIR-FRIED SHRIMP & GINGER —

— SHRIMP IN YELLOW SAUCE —

3 garlic cloves, crushed
1-1/2-inch piece gingerroot, thinly sliced
2 tablespoons vegetable oil
12 to 16 raw large shrimp, peeled, tails on, deveined
2 shallots, finely chopped
Grated peel of ½ lime
2 teaspoons fish sauce
3 tablespoons water
3 green onions, thinly sliced
Lime juice, to serve
Green Onion Brushes, see page 15, to garnish

2 fresh red chiles, seeded, chopped
1 red onion, chopped
1 thick stalk lemon grass, chopped
1-inch piece galangal, chopped
1 teaspoon ground turmeric
1/2 cup water
1 cup coconut milk
14 to 16 raw large shrimp, peeled, deveined
8 Thai basil leaves
2 teaspoons lime juice
1 teaspoon fish sauce
1 green onion, including some green top, cut into thin strips

Using a pestle and mortar or small food processor, pound or mix together garlic and gingerroot into a paste. In a wok, heat oil, add garlic paste and stir-fry 2 to 3 minutes. Stir in shrimp and shallots and stir-fry 2 minutes.

Using a small food processor, mix to a paste chiles, red onion, lemon grass and galangal. Transfer to a wok and heat, stirring, 2 to 3 minutes, then stir in turmeric and water and bring to a boil. Reduce heat and simmer 3 to 4 minutes until most of the water has evaporated.

Stir in lime peel, fish sauce and water. Boil 1 minute until shrimp are pink. Stir in green onions, then remove from heat. Serve in a warm dish sprinkled with lime juice and garnished with onion brushes.

Makes 3 to 4 servings.

Stir in coconut milk and shrimp and simmer, stirring occasionally, about 4 minutes until shrimp are just firm and pink. Stir in basil leaves, lime juice and fish sauce. Sprinkle green onion over shrimp.

Makes 4 servings.

KUNG PO SHRIMP

1 pound prepared raw shrimp
5 or 6 tablespoons water
4 tablespoons cornstarch
2-1/2 cups peanut oil
2 green onions, finely chopped
1/2-inch piece gingerroot, peeled and finely chopped
1 tablespoon rice wine or dry sherry
1 tablespoon light soy sauce
1 teaspoon brown sugar
2 teaspoons sherry vinegar
Sea salt and black pepper

In a bowl, stir water into cornstarch to make a light batter. Dip shrimp in batter to coat evenly; allow excess batter to drain off. In a wok, heat oil until smoking, add shrimp and deep-fry about 3 minutes until golden brown. Using a slotted spoon, remove and then drain on paper towels.

Pour oil from wok, leaving just 2 tablespoonsful. Add green onions and gingerroot and stir-fry 1 minute. Stir in remaining ingredients and bring to a boil. Add shrimp to sauce and heat gently until sauce has thickened.

Makes 4 servings.

SZECHUAN SHRIMP

1 pound shelled uncooked shrimp
2 tablespoons vegetable oil
1 garlic clove, finely chopped
1 small fresh red chile, seeded if desired, finely chopped
1-1/2 teaspoons chili sauce
1/4 teaspoon cornstarch
2 tablespoons Chinese Chicken Stock, see page 22
1/2 teaspoon sea salt
1/4 teaspoon brown sugar

Bring a large saucepan of salted water to a boil, add shrimp, boil for 1 minute then drain. In a wok, heat oil, garlic and chile and stir-fry for 30 seconds. Add chile sauce and stir 3 minutes.

In a small bowl mix together cornstarch, stock, sugar and salt until smooth, then stir into the wok. Bring to a boil, stirring, then simmer until sauce is thick. Add shrimp and gently heat through about 2 minutes.

Makes 4 servings.

—SHRIMP & CUCUMBER CURRY—

1/4 cup coconut cream, see page 10
3 to 4 tablespoons Red Curry Paste, see page 18
8 ounces raw large peeled shrimp
8-inch length cucumber, halved lengthwise, seeded, cut
    into 3/4-inch pieces
1-1/4 cups coconut milk
2 tablespoons tamarind water, see page 12
1 teaspoon crushed palm sugar
Cilantro leaves, to garnish

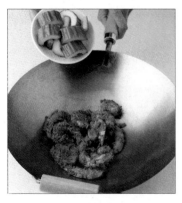

In a wok, heat coconut cream, stirring, until it boils and thickens, and the oil begins to separate. Add the curry paste, and cook, stirring, 3 minutes. Stir in shrimp to coat, then stir in cucumber. Add coconut milk, tamarind water and sugar.

Simmer 3 to 4 minutes until shrimp are pink. Transfer to a warmed serving dish and garnish with cilantro.

Makes 3 servings.

—JASMINE-SCENTED SHRIMP—

3 tablespoons rice wine, sake or dry sherry
1 tablespoon light soy sauce
1-inch piece gingerroot, peeled and finely chopped
1 teaspoon sesame oil
1/4 teaspoon salt
1-1/2 pounds raw medium-size shrimp, shelled and
    deveined
2 tablespoons jasmine or other aromatic tea leaves,
    such as Earl Grey
1/2 cup light fish or chicken stock
2 teaspoons cornstarch dissolved in 1 tablespoon water
1/2 teaspoon sugar
1 tablespoon vegetable oil
4 green onions, thinly sliced
Mint sprigs or jasmine flowers, to garnish

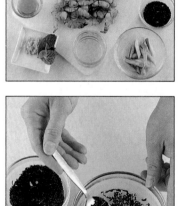

In a medium-size bowl, combine rice wine, sake or dry sherry, soy sauce, gingerroot, sesame oil and salt. Add shrimp and toss to coat well. Let stand 30 minutes, stirring once or twice. In a small bowl, stir the tea leaves into 1/2 cup boiling water and steep 1 minute. Strain tea through a fine tea strainer into another bowl and discard the tea leaves. Add stock to the tea and stir in the cornstarch mixture and sugar.

Heat wok until hot, add vegetable oil and swirl to coat wok. With a Chinese strainer or slotted spoon, remove shrimp from marinade. Working in batches, add shrimp to wok and stir-fry 1 to 2 minutes until pink and firm; remove to a bowl. Stir in green onions and reserved marinade and cook 1 minute. Stir tea mixture and add to wok, cook, stirring, until thickened. Return shrimp to wok and toss lightly to coat. Garnish with mint or jasmine and serve with rice.

Makes 4 servings.

MUSSELS WITH BEANS & CHILE

8 pounds mussels, scrubbed and rinsed
1/2 cup vegetable oil
4 garlic cloves, finely chopped
2 hot red chiles, seeded if desired, finely chopped
1/2 green bell pepper, chopped
3 green onions, sliced
1 teaspoon cornstarch dissolved in 2 teaspoons water
4 tablespoons rice wine or dry sherry
3 tablespoons black bean paste
2 teaspoons ground ginger
1 tablespoon brown sugar
2 tablespoons hot chile paste
3 tablespoons oyster sauce
3 cups Chinese Chicken Stock, see page 22

Place mussels in a large saucepan, add 2 cups water, cover and place over a high flame about 5 minutes, or until the mussels have opened, shaking pan occasionally; this may have to be done in batches. Remove from heat, drain and discard any mussels which have not opened. In a wok, heat oil, add garlic, chiles, green bell pepper and green onions and stir-fry 1 minute.

In a bowl stir together remaining ingredients, stir into wok and bring to a boil, stirring. Simmer until lightly thickened. Add mussels to wok and heat through 5 minutes, occasionally shaking wok.

Makes 4 to 6 servings.

MUSSELS WITH BASIL

1-1/2 pounds mussels in shells, cleaned, debearded and rinsed
1 large garlic clove, chopped
3-inch piece galangal, thickly sliced
2 stalks lemon grass, chopped
10 Thai basil sprigs
1 tablespoon fish sauce
Thai basil leaves, to garnish
Dipping Sauce 1, see page 20, to serve

Place mussels, garlic, galangal, lemon grass, basil sprigs and fish sauce in a large saucepan. Add water to a depth of 1/2 inch. Cover pan, bring to a boil and cook about 5 minutes, shaking pan frequently, until mussels have opened. Discard any mussels that remain closed.

Transfer mussels to a large warmed bowl or individual bowls, and strain cooking liquid over mussels. Garnish with basil leaves. Serve with sauce for dipping.

Makes 2 to 3 servings.

CLAMS WITH SOY & SESAME DIP

-SQUID FLOWERS WITH PEPPERS-

2 pounds clams in shells, scrubbed and rinsed
1 teaspoon sea salt
4 green onions, finely chopped
1-1/2-inch piece gingerroot, peeled and finely chopped
4 tablespoons dark soy sauce
1 teaspoon medium-dry sherry
2 tablespoons sesame oil

Bring a large saucepan of salted water to a rapid boil, add clams and boil for 10 minutes until clams have opened. Discard any clams that do not open.

Drain the clams and remove and discard the top shells.

Sprinkle each clam with green onions and gingerroot. In a bowl mix together the soy sauce, sherry and sesame oil. Spoon a little over each clam.

Makes 4 servings.

2-1/2 cups peanut oil
1 pound cleaned squid
2 slices gingerroot, peeled and finely chopped
1 large green bell pepper, seeded and cut into 1-inch squares
1 teaspoon sea salt
1 tablespoon dark soy sauce
1 teaspoon rice vinegar
1/2 teaspoon brown sugar
Black pepper
1 teaspoon sesame oil

In a wok, heat oil until smoking, add squid and fry 1 minute. Remove and drain on paper towels. Pour oil from wok, leaving just 1 tablespoonful. Add gingerroot and green bell pepper and stir-fry 5 minutes until the bell pepper begins to soften.

Stir in remaining ingredients except sesame oil, bring to a boil, stirring, reduce heat so sauce is simmering, then add squid and gently heat through. Transfer to a warmed serving plate and sprinkle with sesame oil.

Makes 4 servings.

CRAB WON TONS

1/3 cup light soy sauce
2 tablespoons wine vinegar
2 tablespoons sesame oil
1 tablespoon water
1/2 teaspoon crushed dried chiles
2 teaspoons honey or sugar
6 to 8 canned whole water chestnuts, rinsed and minced
2 green onions, finely chopped
1 teaspoon finely chopped gingerroot
8 ounces white crabmeat, drained and picked over
1/2 teaspoon red pepper sauce
1 tablespoon finely chopped fresh cilantro or dill
1 egg yolk
30 won-ton skins
Vegetable oil for deep frying

In a small bowl, mix together 1/4 cup of the soy sauce, vinegar, 1 tablespoon of the sesame oil, water, crushed chiles and honey or sugar. Set aside. In a wok, heat remaining oils, add the water chestnuts, green onions and gingerroot and stir-fry 1 to 2 minutes. Cool slightly, then mix with crabmeat, remaining soy sauce, red pepper sauce, cilantro and egg yolk. Place a teaspoon of mixture in the center of each won-ton skin. Dampen edges with a little water and fold up one corner to opposite corner to form a triangle.

Fold over the bottom 2 corners to meet and press together to resemble a tortellini. Be sure the filling is well-sealed. In the wok, heat 3 inches of vegetable oil to 375F (190C) and deep-fry the won tons in batches 3 minutes or until golden on all sides, turning once during cooking. Remove with a Chinese strainer or slotted spoon to paper towels to drain. Serve with the dipping sauce.

Makes 30 won tons.

DEEP-FRIED CRAB CLAWS

4 large crab claws
10 ounces peeled uncooked shrimp, ground
1/2 teaspoon sea salt
Pinch of white pepper
1 teaspoon cornstarch
1 egg white
1 cup dried white bread crumbs to coat
2½ cups peanut oil

Crack and remove the main shell from each claw, leaving the pincer part intact.

Bring a large saucepan of salted water to a boil. Add crab claws, return to a boil and boil 1 minute. Drain and refresh under cold running water. In a bowl, mash to an even paste the shrimp, salt, pepper, cornstarch and egg white. Divide into 4 portions and press a portion around each claw, leaving pincer showing.

Place bread crumbs on plate, roll claws in bread crumbs to evenly coat. In a wok, heat oil, add claws and fry 10 minutes until golden brown. Drain on paper towels.

Makes 4 servings.

FISH WITH LEMON GRASS

2 tablespoons vegetable oil
1 flat fish, such as sole or flounder (about 1-1/2 pounds), ready to cook
4 garlic cloves, finely chopped
2 fresh red chiles, seeded, finely chopped
1 shallot, chopped
4-1/2 tablespoons lime juice
1/2 teaspoon crushed palm sugar
1-1/2 tablespoons finely chopped lemon grass
2 teaspoons fish sauce
Chile Flower, see page 15, to garnish

In a wok, heat oil, add fish, skin-side down first, and cook 3 to 5 minutes per side until lightly browned and flesh is opaque when tested with a knife. Using a spatula, transfer to a warmed platter, cover and keep warm. Add garlic to wok and fry, stirring occasionally, until browned.

Stir in chiles, shallot, lime juice, sugar, lemon grass and fish sauce. Simmer 1 to 2 minutes. Pour over the fish and garnish with Chile Flower.

Makes 2 servings.

FISH WITH CILANTRO & GARLIC

6 cilantro roots, chopped
3 large garlic cloves, chopped
5 peppercorns, crushed
2 fish fillets, such as trout or flounder
2 pieces banana leaf or foil
3 tablespoons lime juice
1/2 teaspoon crushed palm sugar
1 green onion, finely chopped
1/2 small green chile seeded, thinly sliced
1/2 small red chile, seeded, thinly sliced
Chile Flowers, see page 15, to garnish

Preheat broiler. Using a pestle and mortar or small food processor, pound or mix together cilantro roots, garlic and peppercorns. Spread evenly over inside of fish fillets, then let stand 30 minutes.

Wrap fish in banana leaves or pieces of foil, securing leaf with wooden pick, or folding edges of foil tightly together. Broil about 8 minutes. Meanwhile, in a small bowl, stir together lime juice and sugar, then stir in green onion and chiles. Serve with fish. Garnish with Chile Flowers.

Makes 2 servings.

FISH IN BANANA LEAF CUPS

FISH IN COCONUT SAUCE

3 ounces firm white fish, such as cod or hake, very
  finely chopped
3 ounces peeled shrimp, very finely chopped
2 to 3 teaspoons Red Curry Paste, see page 18
2 tablespoons ground roasted peanuts
1 kaffir lime leaf, finely chopped
2 tablespoons coconut milk
1 egg
2 teaspoons fish sauce
Leafy part of 1/2 Chinese cabbage leaf, finely shredded
2 Banana Leaf Cups, see page 16, if desired
2 teaspoons coconut cream, see page 10
Red chile strips, to garnish

4 tablespoons vegetable oil
1 shallot, chopped
1-1/2-inch piece galangal, finely chopped
2 stalks lemon grass, finely chopped
1 small fresh red chile, seeded, chopped
1/2 cup coconut milk
2 teaspoons fish sauce
5 cilantro sprigs
About 12 ounces white fish fillets, such as halibut or
  red snapper
1 small onion, sliced
Freshly ground pepper

In a bowl, using a fork, mix fish and shrimp together. Mix in curry paste, peanuts and lime leaf. In a small bowl, mix together coconut milk, egg and fish sauce. Stir into fish mixture to evenly combine; set aside 30 minutes.

In a wok, heat 1 tablespoon of the oil over high heat, add shallot, galangal, lemon grass and chile. Stir 3 minutes until lightly colored. Transfer to a small food processor, add coconut milk, fish sauce and cilantro stems (reserve leaves) and process until mixed. Place fish in a heatproof, shallow, round dish. Pour coconut mixture over fish. Cover dish, place over saucepan of boiling water and steam 8 to 10 minutes until fish is opaque when tested with a knife.

Divide cabbage leaf among banana cups or heatproof individual dishes to make a thin layer. Stir fish mixture and divide among cups or dishes. Place in a steaming basket and steam over a saucepan of boiling water. Cover pan and steam about 15 minutes until just set in center. Place on a serving plate, drizzle coconut cream over top and garnish with chile strips.

Meanwhile, heat remaining oil in a wok over medium heat, add onion and cook, stirring occasionally, until browned. Using a slotted spoon, transfer to paper towels. Add reserved cilantro leaves to oil and fry a few seconds. Using a slotted spoon, transfer to paper towels to drain. Scatter fried onions and cilantro leaves over fish and season with plenty of pepper.

Makes 2 servings.

Makes 3 to 4 servings.

—FISH STIR-FRY WITH GINGER—

1/2 cup cornstarch
1/2 teaspoon ground ginger
1 teaspoon ground sea salt
1-1/2 pounds haddock or other firm white fish fillets,
    skinned and cubed
3 tablespoons peanut oil
1-inch piece gingerroot, peeled and finely chopped
4 green onions, thinly sliced
1 tablespoon Chinese black vinegar or red wine vinegar
2 tablespoons rice wine or dry sherry
3 tablespoons dark soy sauce
1 teaspoon sugar
3 tablespoons fresh orange juice

In a bowl, mix together cornstarch, ground ginger and salt, add fish in batches to coat evenly. In a wok, heat oil. Add fish and fry 4 minutes, occasionally turning gently, until evenly browned.

In a bowl, mix together remaining ingredients, stir into wok, reduce the heat so the liquid just simmers, cover and cook 4 minutes.

Makes 4 servings.

—SWEET & SOUR SWORDFISH—

3 tablespoons light soy sauce
2 tablespoons dry sherry or rice wine
3 teaspoons wine vinegar or cider vinegar
1 tablespoon sugar
2 teaspoons chili sauce or tomato ketchup
1 pound swordfish steaks, 1-inch thick
3 tablespoons vegetable oil
1 red bell pepper, cut into 1-inch pieces
1 green bell pepper, cut into 1-inch pieces
4 green onions, cut into 2-inch pieces
1 tablespoon cornstarch, dissolved in 1 tablespoon
    cold water
2/3 cup fish stock or chicken stock
Wild rice mixture, to serve

In a bowl, combine soy sauce, sherry or rice wine, vinegar, sugar and chili sauce or tomato ketchup. Cut swordfish into strips and stir into marinade to coat. Allow to stand 20 minutes. Heat a wok until very hot but not smoking; add 2 tablespoons of the oil and swirl to coat wok. With a slotted spoon, remove fish pieces from the marinade, draining off and reserving as much liquid as possible. Add fish to the wok and stir-fry 2 to 3 minutes, until fish is firm. With a slotted spoon, remove fish strips to a bowl.

Add remaining oil to the wok. Add bell peppers and stir-fry 2 to 3 minutes, until peppers begin to soften. Add green onions and stir-fry 1 more minute. Stir the cornstarch mixture and add the reserved marinade, then stir in the stock until well blended. Pour into the wok and bring to a boil, stirring frequently. Simmer 1 to 2 minutes until thickened. Return swordfish to the sauce and stir gently 1 minute to heat through. Serve with rice.

Makes 4 servings.

—INDONESIAN-STYLE HALIBUT—

——FISH WITH CHILE SAUCE——

4 halibut fillets, about 6 ounces each
Juice of 1 lime
2 teaspoons ground turmeric
1/2 cup vegetable oil
1 garlic clove, finely chopped
1/2-inch piece gingerroot, peeled and finely chopped
1 fresh red hot chile, seeded and chopped
1 onion, sliced lengthwise into thin wedges
2 teaspoons ground coriander
2/3 cup unsweetened coconut milk
1 teaspoon sugar
1/2 teaspoon salt
6 ounces snow peas
Cilantro sprigs, to garnish

1 flat fish, such as flounder or sole (about
    1-1/2 pounds), ready to cook
2 teaspoons vegetable oil plus oil for brushing
3 small dried red chiles, halved lengthwise
2 garlic cloves, finely chopped
1 teaspoon fish sauce
1/3 cup tamarind water, see page 12
1 teaspoon crushed palm sugar

Place fish fillets in a shallow dish. Sprinkle with lime juice and rub the turmeric into both sides of each fillet. Set aside. In a wok, heat half of the oil until hot, but not smoking; swirl to coat wok. Gently slide 2 of the fish fillets into the oil and fry 4 to 5 minutes, carefully turning once during cooking. Remove and drain on paper towels. Add remaining oil to wok and fry remaining fish fillets in the same way. Drain as before and keep fish fillets warm.

Preheat broiler. Brush fish lightly with oil, then broil about 4 minutes per side until lightly colored and flesh is opaque when tested with a knife. Using a spatula, transfer to a warmed platter and keep warm.

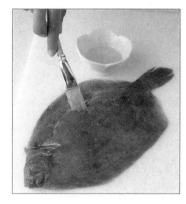

Pour off all but 1 tablespoon oil from wok. Add garlic, gingerroot and chile and stir-fry 1 minute. Add onion and coriander and stir-fry 2 minutes until onion begins to soften. Stir in coconut milk, sugar and salt and bring to a boil, adding a little more water if sauce is too thick. Stir in snow-peas and cook 1 minute, until they turn bright green. Spoon sauce over fish fillets and garnish with cilantro.

Makes 4 servings.

In a small pan, heat the 2 teaspoons vegetable oil, add chiles and garlic and cook 1 minute. Stir in remaining ingredients and simmer 2 to 3 minutes until lightly thickened. Spoon over fish.

Makes 2 servings.

STEAMED SEA BASS

1 (2-1/4-lb.) sea bass, ready to cook with head and tail left on
1 tablespoon rice wine or dry sherry
1 teaspoon sea salt
1 tablespoon peanut oil
2 tablespoons fermented black beans, rinsed, drained and coarsely chopped
1 garlic clove, finely chopped
1/2-inch piece gingerroot, peeled and finely chopped
3 green onions, thinly sliced
2 tablespoons soy sauce
1/2 cup fish stock or chicken stock
6 teaspoons mild Chinese chili sauce
1 teaspoon sesame oil
Cilantro or green onions, to garnish

With a sharp knife, make 3 or 4 diagonal slashes 1/2 inch deep on both sides of fish. Sprinkle inside and out with wine and salt. Place in an oval baking dish which will fit in a wok. Allow to stand 20 minutes. Place a wire rack or 2 inverted ramekins in a wok. Fill wok with 1 inch of water and bring to a boil. Place dish with the fish on the rack or ramekins and cover tightly. Cook 8 to 12 minutes or until fish begins to flake. Remove fish from wok and keep warm. Remove rack or ramekins and pour off water. Wipe wok dry and reheat.

Add peanut oil and swirl to coat wok. Add the black beans, garlic and gingerroot and stir-fry 1 minute. Stir in the green onions, soy sauce and stock and bring to a boil; cook 1 minute. Stir in the chili sauce and sesame oil and remove from the heat. Pour sauce over fish and serve immediately, garnished with cilantro.

Makes 4 servings.

TUNA WITH SPICY SALSA

2 tablespoons sesame oil
1 tablespoon light soy sauce
1 garlic clove, finely chopped
1-1/2 pounds tuna steaks, 1 inch thick, cut into chunks
2 tablespoons vegetable oil
8 ounces daikon, diced
1 small cucumber, peeled, seeded and diced
1 red bell pepper, diced
1 red onion, finely chopped
1 fresh hot red chile, seeded and finely chopped
2 tablespoons lime juice
1 teaspoon sugar
1 tablespoon sesame seeds, toasted
Lime wedges and cilantro sprigs, to garnish
Oriental noodles, to serve

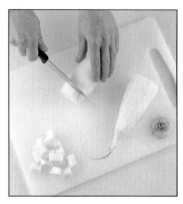

In a shallow dish, combine 1 tablespoon of the sesame oil, soy sauce and garlic. Add tuna chunks and toss gently to coat. Allow to stand 15 minutes. Heat a wok until very hot; add 1 tablespoon of the vegetable oil and swirl to coat. Add daikon, cucumber, bell pepper, onion and chile and stir-fry 2 to 3 minutes or until vegetables begin to soften and turn a bright color. Stir in lime juice, sugar and remaining sesame oil and cook 30 seconds or until sugar dissolves. Remove to a bowl.

Add remaining vegetable oil to wok and, working in batches, if necessary, add fish chunks and stir-fry gently 2 to 3 minutes or until firm. Arrange fish on 4 dinner plates and sprinkle with the sesame seeds. Spoon some of the warm relish onto each plate and garnish with lime wedges and cilantro sprigs. Serve with noodles.

Makes 4 servings.

MONKFISH STIR-FRY

6-inch stalk fresh lemon grass, trimmed
1 teaspoon tomato paste
1 tablespoon vegetable oil
1 tablespoon sesame oil
1 pound monkfish, skinned and cut into chunks or
    1 pound cooked lobster meat
3 garlic cloves, finely chopped
1-inch piece gingerroot, peeled and chopped
1 white onion, cut lengthwise into thin wedges
1 fresh hot red chile, seeded and finely chopped
2 tomatoes, peeled, seeded and chopped
1 teaspoon sugar
2 large green onions, sliced into 1-inch pieces
2 tablespoons chopped cilantro
1 tablespoon lime juice
Lime wedges and cilantro, to garnish

Crush lemon grass and cut into 1-inch pieces. Place in a saucepan with 3/4 cup water and bring to a boil. Simmer 3 minutes. Add tomato paste and stir until dissolved. Set aside. Heat the oils in a wok until very hot. Add fish and stir-fry 3 or 4 minutes or until firm. Transfer fish to a bowl. If using lobster, stir-fry 1 to 2 minutes, then transfer to a bowl. Add garlic and gingerroot to wok and stir-fry 10 seconds. Add white onion and chile and stir-fry 1 to 2 minutes or until onion begins to soften. Add tomatoes, sugar and lemon grass mixture.

Add green onions, chopped cilantro and lime juice; cook 1 minute or until green onions turn bright green. Return fish or lobster to wok and cook 1 minute or until heated through. Serve immediately, garnished with lime and cilantro. Accompany with noodles.

Makes 2 servings.

Note: Monkfish is often called 'poor man's lobster' due to its sweet flavor and firm, lobsterlike texture.

FIVE-SPICE SALMON

1 teaspoon sesame oil
3 tablespoons soy sauce
3 tablespoons dry sherry or rice wine
1 tablespoon honey
1 tablespoon lime juice or lemon juice
1 teaspoon five-spice powder
1-1/2 pounds salmon fillet, skinned and cut into 1-inch
    strips
2 egg whites
1 tablespoon cornstarch
1-1/4 cups vegetable oil
6 green onions, sliced into 2-inch pieces
1/2 cup light fish stock, chicken stock or water
Dash hot pepper sauce (optional)
Lime wedges, to garnish
Cooked rice, to serve

In a shallow baking dish, combine sesame oil, soy sauce, sherry, honey, lime juice and five-spice powder. Add salmon strips and toss gently to coat. Allow to stand 30 minutes. With a slotted spoon, remove the salmon strips from marinade and pat dry with paper towel. Reserve marinade. In a small dish, beat egg whites and cornstarch until soft peaks form. Add salmon strips and toss gently to coat completely.

Heat vegetable oil in the wok until hot. Add the salmon in batches. Fry 2 to 3 minutes until golden, turning once. Remove and drain on paper towels. Pour oil from wok into heatproof bowl and wipe wok clean. Pour marinade into wok and add green onions, stock and pepper sauce, if using. Bring to a boil and simmer 1 to 2 minutes. Add fish and turn gently to coat. Cook 1 minute until hot. Garnish with lime and serve with rice.

Makes 4 servings.

POULTRY

—CHICKEN IN COCONUT MILK—

8 peppercorns
6 cilantro roots, finely chopped
1-3/4-inch piece galangal, thinly sliced
2 fresh green chiles, seeded, thinly sliced
2-1/2 cups coconut milk
Grated peel and juice of 1 lime
4 kaffir lime leaves, shredded
1 (3-lb.) chicken, cut into 8 pieces
1 tablespoon fish sauce
3 tablespoons chopped cilantro leaves to serve

Using a pestle and mortar or small food processor, crush peppercorns, then add cilantro roots and galangal and pound or mix lightly together.

In a wok, briefly heat peppercorn mixture, stirring, then stir in chiles, coconut milk, lime peel and lime leaves. Bring to a simmer, add chicken and simmer 40 to 45 minutes until chicken is very tender and liquid is reduced.

Stir in fish sauce and lime juice. Scatter cilantro leaves over chicken and serve.

Makes 6 to 8 servings.

—CHICKEN WITH CILANTRO—

6 cilantro sprigs
1 tablespoon peppercorns
2 garlic cloves, chopped
Juice of 1 lime
2 teaspoons fish sauce
4 large or 6 medium-size chicken drumsticks or thighs
Lime wedges, to serve
Green Onion Brushes, see page 15, to garnish

Using a pestle and mortar or small food processor, pound or mix together cilantro, peppercorns, garlic, lime juice and fish sauce; set aside.

Using the point of a sharp knife, cut slashes in chicken. Spread spice mixture over chicken; cover and refrigerate 2 to 3 hours, turning occasionally.

Preheat broiler. Broil chicken, basting and turning occasionally, about 10 minutes until golden and cooked through. Serve with lime wedges and garnish with Green Onion Brushes.

Makes 2 to 3 servings.

LEMON GRASS CHICKEN CURRY

12 ounces boneless chicken, chopped into small pieces
1 tablespoon Red Curry Paste, see page 18
3 tablespoons vegetable oil
2 garlic cloves, finely chopped
1 tablespoon fish sauce
2 stalks lemon grass, finely chopped
5 kaffir lime leaves, shredded
1/2 teaspoon crushed palm sugar
1/2 cup water

Place chicken in a bowl, add curry paste and stir to coat chicken; set aside 30 minutes.

In a wok, heat oil, add garlic and fry until golden. Stir in chicken, then fish sauce, lemon grass, lime leaves, sugar and water.

Simmer 15 to 20 minutes until chicken is cooked through. If chicken becomes too dry, add a little more water, but the final dish should be quite dry.

Makes 3 to 4 servings.

BARBECUED CHICKEN

4 fresh red chiles, seeded, sliced
2 garlic cloves, chopped
5 shallots, finely sliced
2 teaspoons crushed palm sugar
1/2 cup coconut cream, see page 10
2 teaspoons fish sauce
1 tablespoon tamarind water, see page 12
4 skinless boneless chicken breasts
Thai basil leaves or cilantro leaves to garnish

Using a pestle and mortar or small food processor, pound or mix together chiles, garlic and shallots to a paste. Work in sugar, then stir in coconut cream, fish sauce and tamarind water.

Using the point of a sharp knife, cut 4 slashes in each chicken breast. Place chicken in a shallow dish and pour spice mixture over chicken. Turn to coat, cover dish and set aside 1 hour.

Preheat broiler. Place chicken on a piece of foil and broil about 4 minutes per side, basting occasionally, until cooked through.

Makes 4 servings.

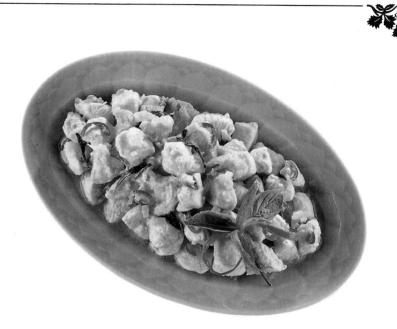

SPICED CHICKEN

CHICKEN WITH BASIL

5 shallots, chopped
3 garlic cloves, chopped
5 cilantro roots, chopped
2 stalks lemon grass, chopped
2 fresh red chiles, seeded, chopped
1-1/2-inch piece gingerroot, finely chopped
1 teaspoon shrimp paste
1-1/2 tablespoons vegetable oil
2 chicken legs, divided into thighs and drumsticks
1-1/2 tablespoons tamarind water, see page 12
1/3 cup water

Using a pestle and mortar, pound to a smooth paste shallots, garlic, cilantro roots, lemon grass, chiles, gingerroot and shrimp paste.

Heat oil in a wok, stir in shallot mixture and cook, stirring 3 to 4 minutes. Stir in chicken pieces to coat evenly.

Add tamarind water and water. Cover and simmer about 30 minutes until chicken is tender. If chicken becomes too dry, add a little more water.

Makes 3 to 4 servings.

2 tablespoons vegetable oil
2 garlic cloves, chopped
12 ounces skinless boneless chicken breasts, finely chopped
1 small onion, finely chopped
3 fresh red chiles, seeded, thinly sliced
20 Thai basil leaves
1 tablespoon fish sauce
1/4 cup coconut milk
Squeeze of lime juice
Chile Flowers, see page 15, and Thai basil leaves to garnish

In a wok, heat 1 tablespoon of the oil, add garlic, chicken, onion and chiles and cook, stirring occasionally, 3 to 5 minutes until cooked through.

Stir in basil leaves, fish sauce and coconut milk. Stir briefly over heat. Add lime juice. Garnish with Chile Flowers and basil leaves.

Makes 2 to 3 servings

—CHICKEN WITH GALANGAL—

1 pound boneless skinless chicken breasts
3 tablespoons vegetable oil
2 garlic cloves, finely chopped
1 onion, quartered, sliced
1-inch piece galangal, finely chopped
8 pieces dried Chinese black mushrooms, soaked 30
    minutes, drained and chopped
1 fresh red chile, seeded, cut into thin strips
1 tablespoon fish sauce
1-1/2 teaspoons crushed palm sugar
1 tablespoon lime juice
12 Thai mint leaves
4 green onions, including some green tops, chopped
3 to 4 tablespoons water
Thai mint leaves to garnish

Using a sharp knife, cut chicken into 2-1/2-inch-long × 1-inch-wide pieces; set aside. In a wok, heat oil, add garlic and onion and cook, stirring occasionally, until golden. Stir in chicken and stir-fry about 2 minutes.

Add galangal, mushrooms and chile and stir-fry 1 minute. Stir in fish sauce, sugar, lime juice, mint leaves, green onions and water. Cook, stirring, about 1 minute. Transfer to a warmed dish and garnish with mint leaves.

Makes 4 servings.

—CHICKEN IN PEANUT SAUCE—

1-inch piece galangal, chopped
2 garlic cloves, chopped
1-1/2 tablespoons Fragrant Curry Paste, see page 19
1/4 cup coconut cream, see page 10
1 pound boneless skinless chicken breast, cut into large
    pieces
2 tablespoons vegetable oil
3 shallots, chopped
1/4 cup roasted peanuts, chopped
2 cups coconut milk
1/2 teaspoon finely chopped dried red chile
2 teaspoons fish sauce
Freshly cooked broccoli to serve

Using a pestle and mortar or small food processor, pound or mix together galangal, garlic and curry paste. Mix in coconut cream. Place chicken in a bowl and stir in spice mixture; set aside 1 hour.

In a wok, heat the oil, add shallots and coated chicken and stir-fry 3 to 4 minutes. In a blender, mix peanuts with coconut milk, then stir into chicken with chile and fish sauce. Simmer about 30 minutes until chicken is tender and sauce is thickened. Transfer to center of a warmed plate and arrange broccoli around chicken.

Makes 4 servings.

—CHICKEN WITH SNOW PEAS—   —YELLOW BEAN CHICKEN—

3 tablespoons vegetable oil
3 garlic cloves, chopped
1 dried red chile, seeded, chopped
3 shallots, chopped
2 tablespoons lime juice
2 teaspoons fish sauce
1/4 cup water
12 ounces chicken, finely chopped
1-1/2 stalks lemon grass, chopped
1 kaffir lime leaf, chopped
6 ounces snow peas
1-1/2 tablespoons coarsely ground browned rice, see
    page 12
3 green onions, chopped
Chopped cilantro leaves to garnish

2 egg whites
4 teaspoons cornstarch
1-1/2 pounds skinless boneless chicken breasts or
    thighs, cut into 1-inch cubes
1/2 cup peanut oil
4 green onions, sliced
2 celery stalks, thinly sliced
1 green bell pepper, diced
1 teaspoon finely chopped gingerroot
1 teaspoon crushed dried chiles
1 teaspoon sugar
4 teaspoons yellow bean paste
4 teaspoons dry sherry or rice wine
1 cup cashew nuts, toasted
Lemon wedges, to serve

In a wok, heat 2 tablespoons of the oil, add garlic and cook, stirring occasionally, until lightly browned. Stir in chile, shallots, lime juice, fish sauce and water. Simmer 1 to 2 minutes, then stir in chicken, lemon grass lime leaf, fish sauce and water. Cook, stirring, for 2 to 3 minutes until chicken is just cooked through. Transfer to a warmed plate and keep warm.

In a medium-size bowl, beat egg whites with the cornstarch. Add chicken cubes, tossing to coat well. Refrigerate 10 to 15 minutes. In a wok, heat peanut oil until very hot and swirl to coat wok. Using a slotted spoon, and work-ing in 2 batches, lift out chicken cubes and add to wok. Stir-fry quickly to keep cubes from sticking. Cook chicken cubes 2 or 3 minutes or until just golden. Remove to paper towels to drain and pour off all but 2 tablespoons oil. (Reserve oil for future frying or discard).

Heat remaining oil in wok, add snow peas and stir-fry for 2 to 3 minutes until just tender. Transfer to a warmed serving plate. Return chicken to wok. Add rice and green onions. Heat for about 1 minute, then transfer to serving plate. Garnish with chop-ped cilantro.

Makes 3-4 servings.

Add green onions, celery, bell pepper and gingerroot and stir-fry 2 or 3 minutes or until onion and bell pepper begin to soften. Stir in the crushed chiles, sugar, yellow bean paste, sherry and cashew nuts, tossing until sugar dissolves. Add chicken cubes and toss to coat; cook 30 seconds. Serve immediately with lemon wedges and accompanied with salad.

Makes 4 servings.

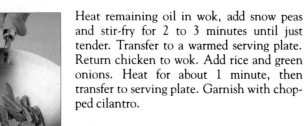

FIVE-SPICE CHICKEN

BANG BANG CHICKEN

2 cups peanut oil
1 tablespoon dark soy sauce
1 tablespoon brandy
1/2 teaspoon five-spice powder
1/2 teaspoon brown sugar
1/2-inch piece gingerroot, peeled and finely chopped
2 green onions, finely chopped
2 garlic cloves, finely chopped
1 pound boned chicken breasts, cubed
1 large egg, beaten
1/2 cup cornstarch

4 tablespoons peanut oil
3 carrots, cut into julienne strips
1 fresh hot red chile, seeded and chopped
1/2 pound bean sprouts, trimmed
1/2 cucumber, seeded and cut into julienne strips
1-3/4 pounds skinned and boned chicken breasts, cut into shreds
1-inch fresh gingerroot, cut in julienne strips
2 garlic cloves, finely chopped
4 green onions, thinly sliced
3 tablespoons cider vinegar or rice vinegar
2 tablespoons dry sherry or rice wine
1 tablespoon sugar
1 teaspoon Chinese chili sauce
2/3 cup chicken stock
3 tablespoons each light soy sauce and tahini

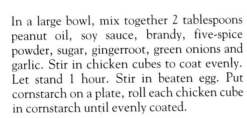

In a large bowl, mix together 2 tablespoons peanut oil, soy sauce, brandy, five-spice powder, sugar, gingerroot, green onions and garlic. Stir in chicken cubes to coat evenly. Let stand 1 hour. Stir in beaten egg. Put cornstarch on a plate, roll each chicken cube in cornstarch until evenly coated.

Heat wok until hot. Add 2 tablespoons of the peanut oil and swirl to coat wok. Add carrots and chile and stir-fry 2 or 3 minutes. Remove to a bowl. Stir-fry bean sprouts 1 minute and remove to bowl. Add cucumber to bowl. Heat remaining oil in wok and add chicken. Working in 2 batches, stir-fry 2 or 3 minutes or until the chicken is white and the juices run clear. Remove to another bowl. Increase heat, add gingerroot and garlic to wok and stir-fry 1 minute. Add green onions and stir-fry 1 minute. Add remaining ingredients and stir-fry until sauce is smooth and thick.

In a wok, heat remaining oil over medium heat, add chicken and deep-fry 4 minutes. Increase heat and fry 2 minutes until golden and cooked through. Using a slotted spoon, lift chicken from oil and drain on paper towels.

Makes 4 servings.

Pour half the sauce over carrot mixture and remaining sauce over chicken; toss each mixture well. Spoon chicken onto center of a serving dish, then spoon vegetables around chicken.

Makes 6 servings.

LEMON CHICKEN

2 egg whites
7 teaspoons cornstarch
1-1/4 pounds skinless boneless chicken breasts, cut
    into thin strips
1/2 cup vegetable oil
1 onion, thinly sliced
1 garlic clove, finely chopped
1 red bell pepper, thinly sliced
2/3 cup chicken stock
Grated peel and juice of 1 lemon
1 tablespoon sugar
1 tablespoon light soy sauce
1 tablespoon rice wine or dry sherry
Dash of hot pepper sauce
Fresh chives, to garnish
Rice, to serve

In a medium-size bowl, beat egg whites with 4 teaspoons cornstarch. Add the chicken strips and toss to coat well. Refrigerate 10 to 15 minutes. In a wok, heat the vegetable oil until very hot and swirl to coat wok. Using tongs or a fork, add the chicken strips, a few at a time. Stir-fry quickly to keep strips from sticking. Cook chicken strips 2 or 3 minutes until just golden. Remove to paper towel to drain and pour off all but 1 tablespoon oil. (Reserve oil for future frying or discard.)

Add onion, garlic and bell pepper to wok. Stir-fry 1 or 2 minutes or until onion begins to soften. Add chicken stock, lemon peel, lemon juice, sugar, soy sauce, wine and hot pepper sauce. Dissolve remaining cornstarch in 2 tablespoons water and stir into the sauce. Cook 30 seconds or until sauce thickens. Add chicken strips and toss to coat. Cook 1 minute or until chicken is heated through. Garnish with chives and serve with rice.

Makes 4 servings.

CHICKEN IN BLACK BEAN SAUCE

1 cup peanut oil
1 pound boned chicken breasts, cubed
10 button mushrooms, halved
1/2 red bell pepper, seeded and diced
1/2 green bell pepper, seeded and diced
4 green onions, finely chopped
2 carrots, thinly sliced
2 tablespoons salted fermented black beans, rinsed
1/2-inch gingerroot, peeled and grated
1 garlic clove, finely chopped
2 tablespoons rice wine or dry sherry
1 cup Chinese Chicken Stock, see page 22
1 tablespoon light soy sauce
2 teaspoons cornstarch dissolved in
    1 tablespoon water

In a wok, heat oil until smoking, add chicken cubes and deep-fry 2 minutes. Using a slotted spoon, lift chicken from oil and drain on paper towels. Pour oil from wok, leaving just 2 tablespoonsful. Add mushrooms to wok and stir-fry 1 minute. Add red and green bell peppers, green onions and carrots, stir-fry 3 minutes.

In a bowl, mash black beans with gingerroot, garlic and rice wine or dry sherry, stir into wok then stir in stock and soy sauce. Cook another 2 minutes. Stir in cornstarch mixture and bring to a boil, stirring. Stir in chicken and heat through gently.

Makes 4 servings.

TANGERINE CHICKEN WINGS

CRISPY-SKIN CHICKEN

1 onion, thinly sliced
1-inch piece gingerroot, peeled and thinly sliced
1 teaspoon sea salt
4 tablespoons dry sherry or rice wine
4 tablespoons soy sauce
16 chicken wings, wing tips removed
1 large tangerine
1/3 cup vegetable oil
2 fresh hot red chiles, seeded and chopped
4 green onions, thinly sliced
2 teaspoons sugar
1 tablespoon white-wine vinegar
1 teaspoon sesame oil
Cilantro sprigs, to garnish

1 (3-lb.) chicken
Salt
1 tablespoon light maple syrup
4 tablespoons plus 1 teaspoon sea salt
3-1/2 teaspoons five-spice powder
2 tablespoons rice vinegar
3-3/4 cups vegetable oil

Bring a large saucepan of salted water to a boil. Add chicken, return to a boil, then remove pan from heat, cover tightly and leave the chicken in the water 30 minutes.

In a large shallow baking dish, combine onion, gingerroot, salt, 1 tablespoon of the sherry and 1 tablespoon of the soy sauce. Add chicken wings and toss to coat well. Let stand 30 minutes. Remove peel from tangerine and slice thinly. Squeeze 2 or 3 tablespoons tangerine juice and reserve. Heat oil in a wok until hot and swirl to coat wok. Remove chicken from the marinade, returning any onion or gingerroot sticking to it. Working in 2 batches, add chicken wings to wok. Fry 3 or 4 minutes or until golden, turning once. Drain on paper towels.

Drain chicken, dry with paper towels and refrigerate 12 hours. In a small bowl, mix together maple syrup, 1 teaspoon salt, 1/2 teaspoon five-spice powder and rice vinegar. Brush over chicken and refrigerate 20 minutes. Repeat until all the coating is used. Refrigerate the chicken at least 4 hours to allow the coating to dry on the skin.

Pour off all but 1 tablespoon oil from wok. Add chiles, green onions and tangerine peel and stir-fry 30 to 40 seconds. Pour in reserved marinade with the onion and gingerroot slices. Add sugar, vinegar and remaining sherry, remaining soy sauce and the tangerine juice. Add the chicken wings and toss to coat well; cook 1 minute or until heated through. Drizzle with sesame oil and garnish with cilantro sprigs. Serve with noodles tossed in sesame oil.

Split chicken in half, through the breast. In a wok, heat oil, add chicken halves and deep-fry 5 minutes until golden brown. Lift chicken from oil and drain on paper towels. Cut into bite-sized pieces. In a small sauce-pan over low heat, stir together remaining sea salt and remaining five-spice powder 2 minutes. Sprinkle over chicken.

Makes 4 servings.

Makes 4 servings.

—SZECHUAN CHICKEN LIVERS—

1 ounce dried Chinese mushrooms or 4 ounces
    mushrooms, quartered
1 teaspoon Szechuan peppercorns
2 tablespoons vegetable oil
1 pound chicken livers, trimmed and cut in half
1-inch piece gingerroot, peeled and finely chopped
2 garlic cloves, finely chopped
4 to 6 green onions, thinly sliced
2 teaspoons cornstarch dissolved in 2 tablespoons
    water
2 tablespoons soy sauce
2 tablespoons rice wine or dry sherry
1/2 teaspoon sugar
Rice, to serve

If using dried mushrooms, place in a bowl,
cover with warm water and soak 20 to 25
minutes. Using a slotted spoon, carefully
remove mushrooms from water, to avoid
disturbing any grit which has sunk to the
bottom. Reserve liquid. Squeeze mushrooms
dry, then cut off and discard stems. Heat wok
until hot. Add Szechuan peppercorns and
dry-fry 2 or 3 minutes or until very fragrant.
Pour into a bowl to cool. When cold, crush in
a mortar and pestle or grind in a spice grinder.
Set aside.

Heat wok until hot. Add oil and swirl to coat
wok. Pat livers dry and stir-fry 2 or 3 minutes.
Add gingerroot, garlic, mushrooms and green
onions. Stir-fry 2 minutes or until livers are
brown. Add 2 tablespoons mushroom liquid
if using dried mushrooms or 2 tablespoons
water if using fresh mushrooms, to dissolved
cornstarch. Stir cornstarch mixture, soy
sauce, wine, ground peppercorns and sugar
into wok. Cook, stirring, until thickened.
Serve with rice.

Makes 4 servings.

—JAPANESE CHICKEN LIVERS—

2 tablespoons light soy sauce
2 tablespoons mirin or dry sherry mixed with 1/2
    teaspoon sugar
1 pound chicken livers, trimmed and cut in half
2 tablespoons vegetable oil
1 green bell pepper, diced
4 green onions, sliced
1 garlic clove, finely chopped
1-inch piece gingerroot, peeled and finely chopped
1/4 teaspoon red (cayenne) pepper
2 tablespoons sugar
3 tablespoons dark soy sauce
1 teaspoon sesame oil
Julienne strips of radish, to garnish (optional)

In a shallow dish, combine light soy sauce,
mirin and chicken livers. Let marinate 20 to
30 minutes, stirring occasionally. Heat a wok
until hot. Add oil and swirl to coat wok.
With a slotted spoon, remove chicken livers
from the marinade and add to wok. Stir-fry 3
or 4 minutes or until beginning to brown.
Add bell pepper, green onions, garlic and
gingerroot and stir-fry 1 or 2 minutes. The
chicken livers should be browned, but still
pink inside.

Stir in cayenne, sugar and dark soy sauce and
toss to coat well. Drizzle with the sesame oil
and serve immediately, garnished with
radish, if desired.

Makes 4 servings.

—DUCK WITH GREEN PEPPERS—

1 egg white
3 tablespoons cornstarch
Sea salt
1 pound boned duck breasts, cubed
2-1/2 cups peanut oil
2 green bell peppers, seeded and cut into 1-inch squares
2 tablespoons light soy sauce
3 teaspoons rice wine or dry sherry
1 teaspoon brown sugar
1/2 cup Chinese Chicken Stock, see page 22
1 teaspoon sesame oil
White pepper

In a bowl, whisk together egg white, cornstarch and 1 teaspoon salt. Stir in duck cubes until coated. Let stand 20 minutes. In a wok, heat peanut oil until very hot. Add duck and deep-fry 4 minutes, until crisp and golden.

Remove duck and drain on paper towels. Add bell peppers to wok and deep-fry 2 minutes, then drain on paper towels. Pour oil from wok, leaving 2 tablespoonsful. Add soy sauce, rice wine or dry sherry, sugar, stock, sesame oil, and salt and pepper to taste. Boil then add cooked duck and bell peppers and gently heat through.

Makes 4 servings.

—DUCK WITH PLUMS—

2 tablespoons vegetable oil
1-1/2 pounds duck breast fillets, skinned and excess fat removed, cut crosswise into thin strips
1/2 pound red plums, pitted and thinly sliced
1/4 cup port
6 teaspoons red-wine vinegar
Grated peel and juice of 1 orange
2 tablespoons Chinese plum sauce or duck sauce
4 green onions, cut into thin strips
1 tablespoon soy sauce
3 or 4 whole cloves
Small piece cinnamon stick
1/2 teaspoon Chinese chili sauce or to taste
Parsley and grated orange peel, to garnish

Heat a wok until hot. Add oil and swirl to coat wok. Add duck strips and stir-fry 3 or 4 minutes or until browned. Remove to a bowl. Add plums, port, vinegar, orange peel, orange juice, plum sauce, green onions, soy sauce, cloves, cinnamon stick and chili sauce to taste. Simmer 4 or 5 minutes or until plums begin to soften.

Return duck strips to wok and stir-fry 2 minutes or until duck is heated through and sauce is thickened. Garnish with parsley and grated orange peel. Serve with noodles.

Makes 4 servings.

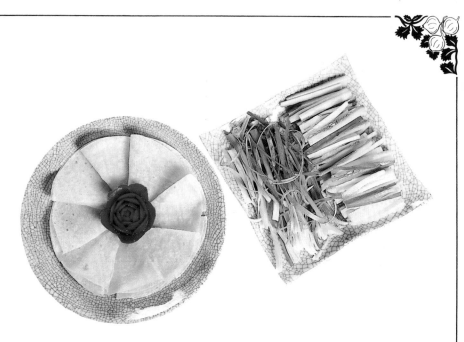

PEKING DUCK

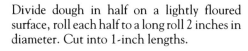

1 (4-lb.) oven-ready duck
1 tablespoon honey
3 tablespoons dark soy sauce
1 tablespoon sesame oil
Red food coloring, if desired
2 tablespoons water
PANCAKES:
3-1/2 cups all-purpose flour
1 cup boiling water
1/3 cup cold water
1 teaspoon sesame oil
TO SERVE:
Hoisin sauce
6 green onions, cut into long shreds
1/2 cucumber, cut into long shreds

Divide dough in half on a lightly floured surface, roll each half to a long roll 2 inches in diameter. Cut into 1-inch lengths.

Place the duck in a colander in the sink. Pour boiling water over; repeat twice. Hang duck overnight in a cold airy place, or place on a rack in the refrigerator. Next morning, in a small bowl, mix together honey, soy sauce, sesame oil and coloring, if used. Place duck on a rack in a roasting pan, making sure the neck opening is closed. Brush evnly with honey mixture and let stand 1 hour. Pre-heat oven to 405F (205C).

Flatten each piece with the palm of the hand. Lightly brush tops with sesame oil and place two pieces together, oiled sides facing. Roll out each pair to 6-inch pancakes.

Stir water into remaining honey mixture and pour through the vent, into the duck. With a meat skewer or wooden skewer, secure vent. Roast duck, 1-1/2 hours, until juices run clear. Remove duck from oven and leave in a warm place 10 minutes before carving.

Meanwhile, make the pancakes. Sift flour into a bowl and gradually stir in boiling water; mix well. Stir in cold water to form a ball. On a floured surface, knead until smooth. Return to bowl, cover with a damp cloth and let stand 15 minutes.

Place a dry, non-stick skillet over medium heat and fry each pancake 20 to 30 seconds until beginning to bubble. Turn over pancake and cook for a further 10 to 15 seconds until light browned. Remove from skillet and carefully separate the top and bottom. Keep warm, interleaved with waxed paper.

Serve the carved duck on a warm plate with the stack of pancakes, and with hoisin sauce, green onions and cucumber in separate bowls.

Makes 4 servings.

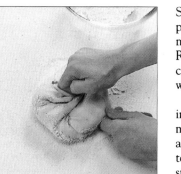

MEAT

LAMB WITH SPINACH

3 tablespoons soy sauce
1/4 teaspoon five-spice powder
1-inch piece gingerroot, peeled and cut into julienne
   strips
2 garlic cloves, finely chopped
1-1/2 pounds lean lamb, cut into thin strips
1 tablespoon sesame oil
1 fresh hot red chile, seeded and thinly sliced
8 green onions, cut into 2-inch pieces
1 mango, peeled and cut into 1/2-inch-thick pieces
6 ounces fresh spinach leaves, washed and dried
3 tablespoons dry sherry or rice wine
1 teaspoon cornstarch dissolved in 1 tablespoon water

LAMB WITH CILANTRO

1 pound lean lamb, cut into thin strips
1 tablespoon cornstarch
1 teaspoon sugar
1 teaspoon sesame oil
2 tablespoons peanut oil
1-3/4 cups broccoli flowerets, sliced
3 dried black winter mushrooms, soaked in hot water
   25 minutes, drained
2 green onions, chopped
1 garlic clove, finely chopped
2 teaspoons rice wine or dry sherry
1 tablespoon dark soy sauce
1 tablespoon finely chopped fresh cilantro

In a shallow baking dish, combine soy sauce, five-spice powder, gingerroot and garlic. Add lamb strips and toss to coat well. Marinate 1 hour, covered, stirring occasionally. Heat a wok until very hot. Add sesame oil and swirl to coat. With a slotted spoon and working in 2 batches, add lamb to wok, draining off and reserving as much marinade as possible. Stir-fry lamb 2 or 3 minutes or until browned on all sides. Remove to a bowl. Add chile to oil remaining in wok and stir-fry 1 minute.

Place lamb in a dish. In a bowl, mix together cornstarch, sugar and sesame oil and spoon over the lamb until well cooked. Let stand 30 minutes.

In a wok, heat peanut oil, add lamb and stir-fry 2 minutes. Remove lamb from wok and keep warm.

Add green onions and mango and stir-fry 1 minute. Stir in spinach leaves, reserved lamb, sherry and reserved marinade. Stir cornstarch mixture and stir into wok. Stir-fry 1 minute, tossing all ingredients until spinach wilts and lamb is lightly glazed with sauce. Serve with noodles.

Makes 4 servings.

Add broccoli, mushrooms, green onions and garlic and stir-fry about 5 minutes until broccoli is just tender. Stir in rice wine or dry sherry, soy sauce, lamb and cilantro. Stir over very high heat 1 minute.

Makes 4 servings.

CHINESE BARBECUED LAMB

2 small eggs, beaten
3/4 cup all-purpose flour
1 teaspoon sea salt
1/2 teaspoon black pepper
1 teaspoon ground Szechuan pepper
4 green onions, finely chopped
2 medium tomatoes, seeded and finely chopped
1 pound lean lamb, cut into cubes
4 teaspoons sesame seeds

In a bowl, mix together all ingredients, except lamb and sesame seeds. Stir in lamb to coat, cover and refrigerate 4 hours.

Preheat broiler or barbecue. Spread sesame seeds on a plate. Roll lamb cubes in sesame seeds to coat evenly.

Thread cubes on to skewers and sprinkle on any remaining sesame seeds. Broil or barbecue 4 or 5 minutes, turning frequently, until cooked.

Makes 4 servings.

HUNAN LAMB STIR-FRY

1 egg white, lightly beaten
2 tablespoons cornstarch
Sea salt and white pepper to taste
1 pound lean lamb, thinly sliced
2-1/2 cups vegetable oil
3 slices gingerroot, peeled and finely chopped
1 (3-oz.) can bamboo shoots, drained and sliced
1 small red bell pepper, seeded and cut into thin strips
3 green onions, finely chopped
1/4 cucumber, cut into strips
2 teaspoons rice wine or dry sherry

In a small bowl, mix together egg white, cornstarch, salt and pepper. Stir lamb slices into mixture to evenly coat. Let stand 30 minutes. In a wok, heat oil, add lamb in batches, keeping slices separate, and deep-fry lamb 2 minutes. Using a slotted spoon, lift lamb from oil and drain on paper towels.

Pour oil from wok, leaving just 2 tablespoonsful. Add gingerroot, bamboo shoots, bell pepper, green onions and cucumber and stir-fry 4 minutes. Add lamb and toss over high heat 1 minute. Stir in rice wine or dry sherry.

Makes 4 servings.

PORK WITH WATER CHESTNUTS

BARBECUED SPARERIBS

1-1/2 tablespoons vegetable oil
4 garlic cloves, chopped
2 fresh red chiles, seeded, finely chopped
12 ounces lean pork, cubed
10 water chestnuts, chopped
1 teaspoon fish sauce
1/4 cup water
Freshly ground pepper
3 tablespoons chopped cilantro
6 green onions, chopped
3 to 4 Green Onion Brushes, see page 15, to garnish

2 tablespoons chopped cilantro stems
3 garlic cloves, chopped
1 teaspoon peppercorns, cracked
1 teaspoon grated lime peel
1 tablespoon Green Curry Paste, see page 18
2 teaspoons fish sauce
1-1/2 teaspoons crushed palm sugar
3/4 cup coconut milk
2 pounds pork spareribs, trimmed
Green Onion Brushes, see page 15, to garnish

In a wok, heat oil, add garlic and chiles and cook, stirring occasionally, until garlic is golden.

Using a pestle and mortar or small food processor, pound or mix together cilantro, garlic, peppercorns, lime peel, curry paste, fish sauce and sugar. Stir in coconut milk. Place spareribs in a shallow dish, pour spiced coconut mixture over ribs, cover and refrigerate 3 hours, basting occasionally.

Stir in pork and stir-fry about 2 minutes until almost cooked through. Add water chestnuts, heat 2 minutes, then stir in fish sauce, water and add plenty of pepper. Stir in cilantro and green onions. Garnish with Green Onion Brushes.

Makes 3 to 4 servings.

Preheat a barbecue or a moderate broiler. Cook ribs about 10 minutes per side until cooked through and browned, basting occasionally with coconut mixture. Garnish with Green Onion Brushes.

Makes 4 to 6 servings.

Note: The ribs can also be cooked on a rack in a roasting pan in an preheated 400F (205C) oven 45 to 60 minutes, basting occasionally.

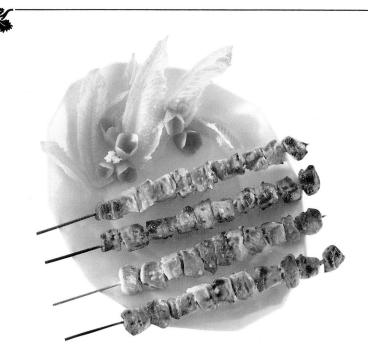

PORK SATAY

12 ounces lean pork, cubed
Juice of 1 lime
1 stalk lemon grass, finely chopped
1 garlic clove, finely chopped
2 tablespoons vegetable oil
SAUCE:
4 tablespoons vegetable oil
1/2 cup raw shelled peanuts
2 stalks lemon grass, chopped
2 fresh red chiles, seeded, sliced
3 shallots, chopped
2 garlic cloves, chopped
1 teaspoon fish paste
2 tablespoons crushed palm sugar
1-1/2 cups coconut milk
Juice of 1/2 lime

Divide pork among 4 skewers and lay in a shallow dish. In a bowl, mix together lime juice, lemon grass, garlic and oil. Pour over pork, turn to coat, cover and refrigerate 1 hour, turning occasionally.

Preheat broiler. Remove pork from dish, allowing excess liquid to drain off. Broil pork, turning frequently and basting, 8 to 10 minutes.

Meanwhile, make sauce. Over a high heat, heat 1 tablespoon of the oil in a wok, add nuts and cook, stirring constantly, 2 minutes. Using a slotted spoon, transfer nuts to paper towels to drain. Using a pestle and mortar or small food processor, grind nuts to a paste. Remove and set aside.

Using a pestle and mortar or small food processor, pound or mix to a smooth paste lemon grass, chiles, shallots, garlic and fish paste.

Heat remaining oil in wok, add spice mixture and cook, stirring, 2 minutes. Stir in peanut paste, sugar and coconut milk. Bring to a boil, stirring. Reduce heat so sauce simmers, add lime juice and simmer, stirring, 5 to 10 minutes, until thickened. Serve in a bowl to accompany pork. Garnish with Carrot Flowers, see page 16, and lettuce leaves.

Makes 4 servings.

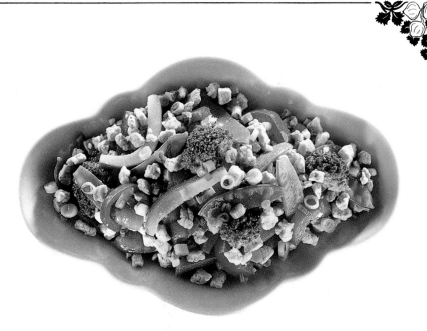

PORK & BAMBOO SHOOTS

2 tablespoons vegetable oil
4 garlic cloves, very finely chopped
12 ounces lean pork, very finely chopped
4 ounces whole bamboo shoots, sliced crosswise
1/4 cup peanuts, coarsely chopped
2 teaspoons fish sauce
Freshly ground pepper
4 large green onions, thinly sliced
Thai basil leaves to garnish

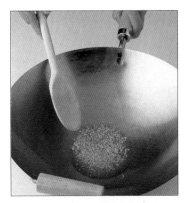

In a wok, heat oil, add garlic and fry, stirring occasionally, about 3 minutes until lightly colored.

Add pork and stir-fry 2 minutes. Add bamboo shoots and cook 1 minute.

Stir in peanuts, fish sauce, plenty of pepper and half of the green onions. Transfer to a warmed serving plate and sprinkle with remaining green onions and the basil leaves.

Makes 4 servings.

VEGETABLES & PORK

8 ounces lean pork, very finely chopped
Freshly ground pepper
2 tablespoons vegetable oil
3 garlic cloves, finely chopped
1 pound prepared mixed vegetables, such as snow peas, broccoli, red bell pepper and zucchini
1 tablespoon fish sauce
1/2 teaspoon crushed palm sugar
1 cup water
3 green onions, finely chopped

In a bowl, mix together pork and plenty of pepper. Set aside 30 minutes.

In a wok or skillet, heat oil, add garlic, cook, stirring occasionally, 2 to 3 minutes, then stir in pork.

Stir briefly until pork changes color. Stir in vegetables, then fish sauce, sugar and water. Stir 3 to 4 minutes until snow peas are bright green and vegetables are crisp-tender. Stir in green onions.

Makes 4 servings.

—PORK WITH GREEN ONIONS—

—COCONUT PORK WITH LIME—

2-1/2 cups coconut milk
1 pound lean pork, cut into 1-inch cubes
1 tablespoon fish sauce
1/2 teaspoon crushed palm sugar
1 cup raw shelled peanuts, skins removed
3 fresh red chiles, seeded, chopped
1-1/2-inch piece galangal, chopped
4 garlic cloves
1 stalk lemon grass, chopped
1/4 cup coconut cream, see page 10
8 green onions, chopped
2 pounds spinach
Warmed coconut cream and roasted peanuts, to serve

6 pork cutlets, about 4 ounces each
1/2-inch piece gingerroot, peeled and grated
2 teaspoons ground cumin
1 teaspoon ground coriander
1 teaspoon chili powder to taste
1 teaspoon paprika
1/2 teaspoon salt
2 tablespoons vegetable oil
1 onion, cut lengthwise into thin wedges
3 or 4 garlic cloves, finely chopped
1-1/4 cups unsweetened coconut milk
Grated peel and juice of 1 large lime
1 small bok choy, shredded
Lime slices and cilantro leaves, to garnish
Noodles, to serve

In a wok, heat coconut milk to a simmer, lower heat so liquid barely moves, add pork and cook about 25 minutes until very tender. Meanwhile, using a small food processor mix fish sauce, sugar, raw peanuts, chiles, galangal, garlic and lemon grass to a paste. In another wok or a skillet, heat coconut cream until the oil separates. Add green onions and peanut paste and cook, stirring frequently, 2 to 3 minutes.

Place cutlets between 2 sheets of waxed paper. Pound to 1/4 inch thickness. Cut pork into strips. In a large shallow dish, combine gingerroot, cumin, coriander, chili powder, paprika and salt. Stir in pork strips and let stand 15 minutes. Heat a wok until very hot. Add oil and swirl to coat wok. Add pork and stir-fry 2 or 3 minutes or until cooked through. Remove to a plate and keep warm. Pour off all but 1 tablespoon oil from the wok.

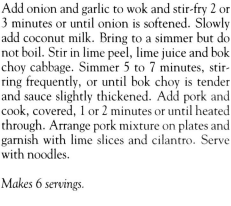

Stir in milk from pork and boil until slightly thickened. Pour over pork, stir and cook 5 minutes more. Rinse spinach leaves, then pack into a pan with just water left on them. Gently cook about 3 minutes until just warmed. Arrange on a warmed serving plate. Spoon pork and sauce onto center. Drizzle with warmed coconut cream and sprinkle with roasted peanuts.

Makes 4 to 6 servings.

Add onion and garlic to wok and stir-fry 2 or 3 minutes or until onion is softened. Slowly add coconut milk. Bring to a simmer but do not boil. Stir in lime peel, lime juice and bok choy cabbage. Simmer 5 to 7 minutes, stirring frequently, or until bok choy is tender and sauce slightly thickened. Add pork and cook, covered, 1 or 2 minutes or until heated through. Arrange pork mixture on plates and garnish with lime slices and cilantro. Serve with noodles.

Makes 6 servings.

PORK WITH MELON & MANGO

1 small cantaloupe or 1/2 Honeydew melon, cut into
   thin strips
1 slightly under-ripe mango, peeled and cut into thin
   strips
Salt and freshly ground pepper
1 tablespoon sugar
Juice of 1 lime or lemon
2 tablespoons sesame oil
1/2 pound pork tenderloin, cut into shreds
4 to 6 green onions, thinly sliced
2 garlic cloves, finely chopped
5 tablespoons nam pla (fish sauce)
1 tablespoon cider vinegar
1/2 teaspoon crushed dried chiles
Chopped peanuts and chopped cilantro, to garnish

In a medium-size bowl, toss melon and
mango strips with salt, pepper, sugar and lime
juice. Set aside. Heat a wok until very hot.
Add oil and swirl to coat wok, add shredded
pork and stir-fry 2 or 3 minutes or until
golden. With a slotted spoon, remove to
paper towels and drain.

To the oil remaining in the wok, add green
onions and garlic and stir-fry 1 minute. Stir in
the nam pla, vinegar and crushed chiles. Add
the reserved pork and the melon mixture,
together with any juices. Toss to mix ingredients and heat through. Spoon onto a
shallow serving dish and sprinkle with chopped peanuts and cilantro. Serve hot or warm
with noodles or shredded Chinese cabbage.

Makes 2 servings.

INDONESIAN-STYLE PORK

1 tablespoon all-purpose flour, seasoned
1-1/4 pounds pork tenderloin, cut into small cubes
2 or 3 tablespoons vegetable oil
1 onion, cut lengthwise in half and thinly sliced
2 garlic cloves, finely chopped
1-inch piece gingerroot, peeled and cut into julienne
   strips
1/2 teaspoon sambal oelek (see Note) or Chinese chili
   sauce
1/4 cup Indonesian soy sauce or dark soy sauce
   sweetened with 1 tablespoon sugar
Cilantro leaves, to garnish

In a bowl, combine seasoned flour and pork;
toss to coat. Shake to remove excess flour.

Heat a wok until very hot. Add 2 tablespoons
of the oil and swirl to coat wok. Add pork
cubes and stir-fry 3 or 4 minutes or until
browned on all sides, adding a little more oil
if necessary. Push pork to one side and add
onion, garlic and gingerroot and stir-fry 1
minute, tossing all the ingredients.

Add sambal oelek, soy sauce and 2/3 cup
water; stir. Bring to a boil, then reduce heat
to low and simmer, covered, 20 to 25
minutes, stirring occasionally, or until pork is
tender and sauce thickened. Garnish with
cilantro and serve with fried rice.

Makes 4 servings.

Note: Sambal oelek is a very hot, chile-based
Indonesian condiment available in speciality
or oriental food shops.

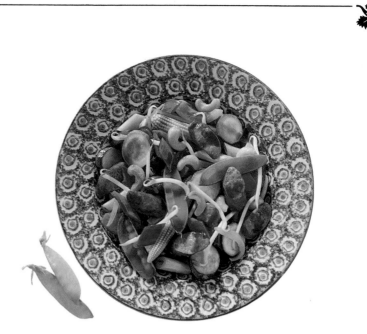

BARBECUED PORK

CHINESE SAUSAGE STIR-FRY

1 (1-1/2-lb.) pork loin, cut into long strips
2/3 cup brown sugar
3 tablespoons boiling water
1 tablespoon dark soy sauce
1 tablespoon oyster sauce
2 tablespoons rice wine or dry sherry
1 teaspoon sesame oil
1/2 teaspoon sea salt
1/2 teaspoon red food coloring, if desired
Chinese shredded lettuce, to serve

2 tablespoons sesame oil or vegetable oil
1/2 pound Chinese sausage (see Note) or sweet Italian-style sausage, cut diagonally into thin slices
1 onion, cut in half lengthwise and sliced
1 red bell pepper, diced
4 ounces canned baby corn-on-the-cobs
2 zucchini, thinly sliced
4 ounces snow peas
8 green onions, cut into 1-inch pieces
1 ounce bean sprouts, rinsed and drained
1/4 cup cashew nuts or peanuts
2 tablespoons soy sauce
3 tablespoons dry sherry or rice wine
Rice or noodles, to serve

Place pork in a medium bowl. In a small bowl, stir together sugar and boiling water until sugar dissolves, then stir in remaining ingredients except lettuce. Cool slightly, then pour over pork, turning pork several times to coat evenly. Refrigerate 8 hours, turning the pork several times. Lift pork from marinade, allowing excess to drain off; reserve. Preheat broiler or barbecue.

Heat a wok until hot. Add oil and swirl to coat wok. Add sausage slices and stir-fry 3 or 4 minutes or until browned and cooked. Add onion, bell pepper and baby corn and stir-fry 3 minutes. Add zucchini, snow peas and green onions and stir-fry 2 minutes.

Thread meat onto meat skewers and barbecue or broil about 8 minutes until crisp and cooked, basting several times with reserved marinade. To serve, remove the pork from the skewers, cut into bite-sized pieces and serve on a bed of shredded Chinese lettuce.

Makes 4 to 6 servings.

Stir in the bean sprouts and nuts and stir-fry 1 or 2 minutes. Add soy sauce and dry sherry and stir-fry 1 minute or until vegetables are tender but still crisp and sausage slices completely cooked through. Serve with rice or noodles.

Makes 4 servings.

Note: Chinese sausage is available in Chinese groceries and some speciality shops and must be cooked before eating.

TERIYAKA STEAKS

1/4 cup mirin or dry sherry sweetened with
   1 teaspoon sugar
1/4 cup light soy sauce
1/2-inch piece gingerroot, peeled and minced
1 garlic clove, finely chopped
1 teaspoon sugar
1/2 teaspoon red pepper sauce or to taste
4 beef sirloin or tenderloin steaks, cut into strips
2 tablespoons sesame oil
4 green onions, thinly sliced
Cilantro leaves, to garnish
Marinated cucumbers and rice, to serve

In a shallow baking dish, combine mirin, soy
sauce, gingerroot, garlic, sugar and red
pepper sauce to taste.

Add the meat and turn to coat well. Let stand
1 hour, turning strips once or twice.

Heat a wok until very hot. Add sesame oil
and swirl to coat wok. Drain meat, reserving
marinade, and add to wok. Stir-fry 2 or 3
minutes or until browned on all sides. Add
marinade and green onions. Cook 3 to 5
minutes or until meat is cooked to desired
doneness and most of marinade has evaporated, glazing the meat. Garnish with cilantro
and serve with marinated cucumbers and
rice.

Makes 4 servings.

SPICY BEEF WITH PEPPERS

1 tablespoon cornstarch
1/4 cup water
1/4 cup light soy sauce
1 tablespoon honey or brown sugar
1 teaspoon Chinese chili sauce
2 tablespoons vegetable oil
1 pound beef round or sirloin steak, cut crosswise into
   thin strips
1 tablespoon sesame oil
2 garlic cloves, finely chopped
1 fresh hot red chile, seeded and thinly sliced
1 onion, thinly sliced
1 each red, green and yellow bell pepper, cut into
   thin strips
Rice, to serve

In a small bowl, dissolve cornstarch in the
water. Stir in soy sauce, honey and chili sauce
until blended. Set aside. Heat a wok until
very hot. Add vegetable oil and swirl to coat
wok. Add beef strips and stir-fry 2 or 3
minutes or until beef is browned. With a
slotted spoon, remove beef to a bowl.

Add sesame oil to the wok and add garlic and
chile. Stir-fry 1 minute or until fragrant. Add
onion and bell pepper strips and stir-fry 2 or 3
minutes or until beginning to soften. Stir
cornstarch mixture, then stir into mixture in
wok and stir until sauce bubbles and begins to
thicken. Add beef strips and any juices and
stir-fry 1 minute or until beef is heated
through. Serve with rice.

Makes 4 servings.

BEEF IN OYSTER SAUCE

1 tablespoon cornstarch
1-1/2 tablespoons soy sauce
1-1/2 tablespoons rice wine or dry sherry
1 pound beef round, sirloin or tenderloin steak, cut crosswise into thin strips
2 tablespoons sesame oil
1/2-inch piece gingerroot, peeled and chopped
2 garlic cloves, finely chopped
4 stalks celery, sliced
1 red bell pepper sliced
4 ounces mushrooms, sliced
4 green onions, sliced
2 tablespoons oyster sauce
1/2 cup chicken stock or water
White and wild rice mixture, to serve

DRY-FRIED BEEF STRIPS

2 tablespoons sesame oil
1 pound beef round or sirloin steak, cut crosswise into julienne strips
2 tablespoons rice wine or dry sherry
1 tablespoon light soy sauce
2 garlic cloves, finely chopped
1/2-inch piece gingerroot, peeled and finely chopped
1 tablespoon Chinese hot bean sauce
2 teaspoons sugar
1 carrot, cut into julienne strips
2 celery stalks, cut into julienne strips
2 or 3 green onions, thinly sliced
1/4 teaspoon ground Szechuan pepper
White and wild rice mixture, to serve

In a bowl, combine 2 teaspoons of the cornstarch with soy sauce and sherry. Add beef strips and toss to coat well. Let stand 25 minutes. Heat a wok until very hot. Add oil and swirl to coat wok. Add beef strips and stir-fry 2 or 3 minutes or until browned. With a slotted spoon, remove to a bowl. Add gingerroot and garlic to oil remaining in wok and stir-fry 1 minute. Add celery, bell pepper, mushrooms and green onions and stir-fry 2 or 3 minutes or until vegetables begin to soften.

Heat a wok until very hot. Add oil and swirl to coat wok. Add beef and stir-fry 15 seconds to quickly seal meat. Add 1 tablespoon of the rice wine and stir-fry 1 or 2 minutes or until beef is browned. Pour off and reserve any excess liquid and continue stir-frying until beef is dry.

Stir in oyster sauce and combine remaining cornstarch with the stock, then stir into mixture in wok and bring to a boil. Add reserved beef strips and cook, stirring, 1 minute or until sauce bubbles and thickens and beef is heated through. Serve with rice.

Makes 4 servings.

Stir in soy sauce, garlic, gingerroot, bean sauce, sugar, remaining rice wine and any reserved cooking juices and stir to blend well. Add carrot, celery, green onions and ground Szechuan pepper and stir-fry until the vegetables begin to soften and all the liquid is absorbed. Serve with rice.

Makes 4 servings.

THAI BEEF WITH NOODLES

1/4 cup rice wine or dry sherry
2 tablespoons light soy sauce
2 garlic cloves, finely chopped
1-inch piece fresh gingerroot, peeled and finely
    chopped
1/2 teaspoon dried crushed chiles
1 pound sirloin or tenderloin steak, 1-inch thick, cut
    crosswise into 1/2-inch strips
12 ounces ramen noodles or thin spaghetti
1 tablespoon sesame oil
4 ounces snow peas
4 to 6 green onions, cut into 2-inch pieces
2 teaspoons cornstarch, dissolved in 1/4 cup water
2 tablespoons chopped cilantro
Cilantro leaves and lime slices, to garnish

In a shallow baking dish, combine rice wine, soy sauce, garlic, gingerroot and chiles. Add steak to dish and marinate 30 minutes, covered, turning once. Cook noodles according to package directions, drain and set aside. Heat wok until very hot. Add sesame oil and swirl to coat wok. Remove steak from marinade, scraping off any gingerroot and garlic and reserving marinade. Pat steak dry with paper towels. Add steak to wok and stir-fry 4 minutes or until browned. Remove and keep warm.

Add snow peas and green onions to any oil remaining in wok and stir-fry 1 minute. Stir cornstarch mixture and stir into wok with reserved marinade Bring to a boil, stirring. Add reserved noodles and chopped cilantro. Add beef. Toss to coat well. Divide among 4 plates. Garnish with cilantro leaves and lime slices.

Makes 4 servings.

SPICY SESAME BEEF

1 tablespoon cornstarch
3 tablespoons light soy sauce
1 pound beef sirloin steak, cut crosswise into thin strips
12 ounces broccoli
2 tablespoons sesame oil
1-inch piece gingerroot, peeled and cut into julienne
    strips
2 garlic cloves, finely chopped
1 fresh hot red chile, seeded and thinly sliced
1 red bell pepper, thinly sliced
1 (14-oz.) can baby corn on-the-cob, drained
1/2 cup beef stock, chicken stock or water
4 to 6 green onions, cut into 2-inch pieces
Toasted sesame seeds, to garnish
Noodles or rice, to serve

In a bowl, combine cornstarch and soy sauce. Add beef strips and toss to coat well. Let stand 20 minutes. Cut large flowerets from the broccoli and divide into small flowerets. With a vegetable peeler, peel the stalk and cut diagonally into 1-inch pieces. Heat a wok until very hot. Add sesame oil and swirl to coat. Add beef strips and marinade and stir-fry 2 or 3 minutes or until browned.

With a slotted spoon, remove beef strips to a bowl. Add gingerroot, garlic and chile to the wok and stir-fry 1 minute. Add broccoli, bell pepper and baby corn and stir-fry 2 or 3 minutes or until broccoli is tender but still crisp. Add the stock and stir 1 minute or until sauce bubbles and thickens. Add green onions and reserved beef strips and stir-fry 1 or 2 minutes or until beef strips are heated through. Sprinkle with sesame seeds and serve with noodles or rice.

Makes 4 servings.

RICE & NOODLES

EGG FRIED RICE

3/4 cup long-grain rice
3 eggs, beaten
2 tablespoons vegetable oil
1 garlic clove, finely chopped
3 green onions, finely chopped
3/4 cup cooked or thawed frozen green peas
1 tablespoon light soy sauce
1 teaspoon sea salt

Cook rice according to package directions until tender but still firm to the bite. In a small saucepan, cook eggs over medium-low heat, stirring until lightly scrambled. Remove and keep warm.

In a wok, heat oil, add garlic, green onions and peas and stir-fry 1 minute. Stir in rice to mix thoroughly.

Add soy sauce, eggs and salt. Stir to break up egg and mix thoroughly.

Makes 4 servings.

GREEN FRIED RICE

3/4 cup long-grain rice
3 eggs, beaten
4 tablespoons vegetable oil
8 ounces spring greens or young spinach, ribs removed
  and finely sliced
1 garlic clove, finely chopped
4 green onions, finely chopped
1/2 cup ham, shredded

Cook rice according to package directions until tender but still firm to the bite. Use eggs to make an omelet, then cut it into thin strips.

In a wok, heat 1 tablespoon vegetable oil, add greens or spinach and fry 1 minute; remove and keep warm.

Add remaining oil to the work, add garlic and green onions and stir-fry 1 minute, then stir in the rice. When mixed thoroughly, stir in ham, greens, omelet slices and salt.

Makes 4 servings.

CRAB FRIED RICE

3/4 cup long-grain rice
3 eggs, beaten
1 (3-oz.) can crab meat
2 tablespoons vegetable oil
2-1/3 cups bean sprouts
1 tablespoon light soy sauce
6 green onions, finely chopped
1 teaspoon sesame oil

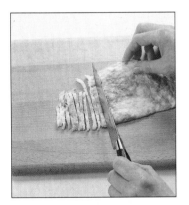

Cook rice according to package directions until tender but still firm to the bite. In a bowl mix together eggs and crab meat with its liquid. Use to make an omelet, then cut it into strips.

In a wok, heat vegetable oil, add bean sprouts and fry 1 minute. Remove from wok and keep warm.

Add rice to wok and stir-fry 3 mintues. Stir in soy sauce and cook 2 minutes. Stir in bean sprouts, omelet strips and green onions, and cook 2 to 3 minutes. Serve sprinkled with sesame oil.

Makes 4 servings.

YANG CHOW FRIED RICE

3/4 cup long-grain rice
3 tablespoons peanut oil
2 medium onions, finely sliced
3 slices gingerroot, peeled and finely chopped
1/2 cup ground pork
1 tablespoon light soy sauce
1 teaspoon brown sugar
½ teaspoon sea salt
2 eggs, beaten
3 dried black winter mushrooms, soaked in hot water
  25 minutes, drained and squeezed
2 large tomatoes, peeled, seeded and chopped
1/3 cup cooked or thawed frozen green peas

Cook rice according to package directions until tender but still firm to the bite. In a wok, heat oil, add onion and gingerroot and stir-fry 2 minutes. Stir in pork, continue stirring 3 minutes until crisp, then add soy sauce and sugar. Stir-fry 1 minute, then stir in rice. Remove to a warmed dish and keep warm.

Pour eggs into wok, season with salt and pepper, then cook stirring 2 to 3 minutes until just beginning to set. Stir in mushrooms, tomatoes and peas. Cook 2 to 3 minutes, then stir in rice mixture.

Makes 4 servings.

THAI FRIED RICE

3/4 cup long-grain white rice
4 ounces long beans or green beans, cut into 1-inch
   lengths
3 tablespoons vegetable oil
2 onions, finely chopped
3 garlic cloves, crushed
3 ounces lean pork, very finely chopped
3 ounces boneless skinless chicken breast, very finely
   chopped
2 eggs, beaten
2 tablespoons Nam Prik, see page 19
1 tablespoon fish sauce
3 ounces cooked peeled shrimp
Cilantro leaves, shredded
Green onions and lime wedges to garnish

SPICY FRIED RICE

3/4 cup long-grain white rice
2 tablespoons vegetable oil
3 garlic cloves, chopped
1 large onion, finely chopped
2 fresh green chiles, seeded, finely chopped
2 tablespoons Red Curry Paste, see page 18
2 ounces lean pork, very finely chopped
3 eggs, beaten
1 tablespoon fish sauce
1/3 cup cooked peeled shrimp
Thinly sliced red chile, shredded cilantro leaves and
   Green Onion Brushes, see page 15, to garnish

Cook rice, see page 12. Add beans to a pan of boiling water and cook 2 minutes. Drain and refresh under cold running water. Drain well. In a wok, heat oil, add onions and garlic and cook, stirring occasionally, until softened. Stir in pork and chicken and stir-fry 1 minute. Push to side of wok.

Cook rice, see page 12. Heat oil in a wok, add onion, garlic and chiles and cook, stirring occasionally, until onion has softened. Stir in curry paste and cook, stirring, 4 minutes. Add pork and stir-fry 2 to 3 minutes. Stir in rice to coat with ingredients, then push to side of wok.

Pour eggs into center of wok. When just beginning to set, stir in pork mixture followed by Nam Prik, fish sauce and rice. Stir 1 to 2 minutes, then add beans and shrimp. Garnish with cilantro leaves, green onions and lime wedges.

Makes 4 servings.

Pour eggs into center of wok. When just beginning to set, stir into the rice, adding fish sauce at the same time. Stir in shrimp, then transfer rice mixture to a warmed serving dish and garnish with chile, cilantro and onion brushes.

Makes 4 servings.

THAI RICE NOODLES

RICE, CHICKEN & MUSHROOMS

8 ounces flat rice noodles
3 tablespoons vegetable oil
2 garlic cloves, chopped
1 red bell pepper, thinly sliced
1 tablespoon soy sauce
1 teaspoon Chinese chili sauce
2 tablespoons nam pla (fish sauce)
4 teaspoons white-wine vinegar
1 tablespoon brown sugar
1 pound cooked peeled shrimp
6 ounces bean sprouts
6 green onions, thinly sliced
1/4 cup sesame oil
3 tablespoons chopped peanuts, to garnish

3/4 cup long-grain white rice
2 tablespoons vegetable oil
1 small onion, finely chopped
2 garlic cloves, finely chopped
2 fresh red chiles, seeded, cut into slivers
8 ounces boneless skinless chicken breasts, finely
    chopped
3 ounces bamboo shoots, chopped
8 pieces dried Chinese black mushrooms, soaked 30
    minutes, drained and chopped
2 tablespoons dried shrimp
1 tablespoon fish sauce
About 25 Thai basil leaves
Thai basil leaves to garnish

Place noodles into a large heatproof bowl. Add enough hot water to cover noodles by 2 inches and let stand 15 minutes or until softened. Drain and set aside. Heat a wok until very hot. Add vegetable oil and swirl to coat wok. Add garlic and bell pepper and stir-fry 3 minutes or until pepper is crisp-tender. Add noodles, soy sauce, chili sauce, nam pla, vinegar and sugar and stir-fry 1 minute. Add a little water if noodles begin to stick.

Cook rice, see page 12. Heat oil in a wok, add onion and garlic and cook, stirring occasionally, until golden. Add chiles and chicken and stir-fry 2 minutes.

Stir in shrimp, bean sprouts, green onions and sesame oil and stir-fry 2 or 3 minutes until shrimp are hot. Sprinkle with peanuts and serve hot.

Makes 4 servings.

Stir in bamboo shoots, mushrooms, dried shrimp and fish sauce. Stir-fry 2 minutes, then stir in rice and the 25 basil leaves. Garnish with additional basil leaves.

Makes 4 servings.

COCONUT NOODLES

8 ounces whole-wheat spaghetti or linguine
4 tablespoons peanut oil
4 ounces shiitake or oyster mushrooms, cut in halves
1 red bell pepper, thinly sliced
1/2 small Chinese cabbage, shredded
4 ounces snow peas, thinly sliced
4 to 6 green onions, thinly sliced
3/4 cup unsweetened coconut milk
2 tablespoons rice wine or dry sherry
1 tablespoon soy sauce
1 tablespoon oyster sauce
1 teaspoon Chinese chili sauce
1 tablespoon cornstarch dissolved in 2 tablespoons
    water
1/2 cup chopped fresh mint or cilantro
Mint sprig, to garnish

In a large saucepan of boiling water, cook pasta according to package directions. Drain pasta, turn into a large bowl and toss with 1 tablespoon of the oil. Heat a wok until hot. Add remaining oil and swirl to coat wok. Add mushrooms, bell pepper and cabbage and stir-fry 3 minutes or until vegetables begin to soften. Stir in noodles, snow peas and green onions; stir-fry 1 minute.

Slowly add coconut milk, wine, soy sauce, oyster sauce and chili sauce and bring to a simmer. Stir cornstarch mixture and, pushing ingredients to one side, add to wok. Stir to combine liquid ingredients, then stir in chopped mint. Stir-fry 3 minutes or until heated through. Garnish with mint.

Makes 4 servings.

NOODLES WITH HERB SAUCE

1/2 cup vegetable oil
2 tablespoons raw shelled peanuts
1 small green chile, seeded, sliced
3/4-inch piece galangal, chopped
2 large garlic cloves, chopped
Leaves from 1 bunch Thai basil (about 90)
Leaves from 1 small bunch Thai mint (about 30)
Leaves from 1 small bunch cilantro (about 45)
2 tablespoons lime juice
1 teaspoon fish sauce
12 to 16 ounces egg noodles, soaked 5 to 10 minutes

Over high heat, heat oil in a wok, add peanuts and cook, stirring, about 2 minutes, until browned. Using a slotted spoon, transfer nuts to paper towels to drain; reserve oil.

Using a small food processor, coarsely grind peanuts. Add chile, galangal and garlic. Mix briefly. Add herbs, lime juice, fish sauce and reserved oil. Drain noodles, shake to loosen, then cook in boiling salted water 2 minutes, until soft. Drain well, turn into a warmed dish and toss with sauce.

Makes 4 servings.

CRISPY NOODLES

6 ounces rice vermicelli
6 pieces dried Chinese black mushrooms
4 ounces lean pork
4 ounces chicken breast
Vegetable oil for deep-frying
2 eggs
4 garlic cloves, finely chopped
3 shallots, thinly sliced
1 fresh red chile, seeded and sliced
1 fresh green chile, seeded and sliced
6 tablespoons lime juice
1 tablespoon fish sauce
1 tablespoon crushed palm sugar
1-1/2 ounces peeled cooked shrimp
4 ounces bean spouts
3 green onions, thickly sliced

Add enough oil to wok for deep-frying. Heat to 375F (190C). Add noodles in batches and fry until puffed, light golden-brown and crisp. Transfer to paper towels. Set aside.

Soak vermicelli in water 20 minutes, then drain and set aside. Soak mushrooms in water 20 minutes, drain, chop and set aside. Cut pork and chicken into cubes or 1-inch strips. Set aside.

Pour off oil leaving 3 tablespoons. Add garlic and shallots and cook, stirring occasionally, until lightly browned. Add pork, stir-fry 1 minute, then stir in chicken and stir-fry 2 minutes. Stir in chiles, mushrooms, lime juice, fish sauce and sugar.

For garnish, heat 2 teaspoons vegetable oil in a wok. In a small bowl, beat eggs with 2 tablespoons water, then drip small amounts in batches in tear shapes onto wok. Cook 1-1/2 to 2 minutes until set. Remove using a thin spatula. Set aside.

Boil until liquid becomes slightly syrupy. Add shrimp, bean sprouts and noodles, tossing to coat with sauce without breaking up noodles. To serve, garnish with green onions and egg tear shapes.

Makes 4 servings.

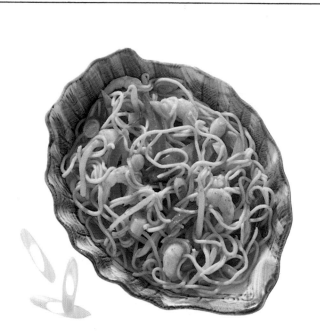

CHOW MEIN

SINGAPORE NOODLES

3 tablespoons soy sauce
2 tablespoons dry sherry or rice wine
1 teaspoon Chinese chili sauce
1 tablespoon sesame oil
2 tablespoons cornstarch
12 ounces skinless boneless chicken breasts, shredded
8 ounces Chinese long noodles or linguine
2 tablespoons vegetable oil
2 celery stalks, thinly sliced
6 ounces button mushrooms
1 red or green bell pepper, thinly sliced
4 ounces snow peas
4 to 6 green onions, thinly sliced
1/2 cup chicken stock or water
4 ounces bean sprouts

8 ounces thin round noodles
1/4 cup vegetable oil
2 garlic cloves, chopped
1-inch piece gingerroot, peeled and finely chopped
1 fresh hot red chile, seeded and chopped
1 red bell pepper, thinly sliced
4 ounces snow peas, sliced if large
4 to 6 green onions, thinly sliced
6 ounces peeled cooked shrimp
4 ounces bean sprouts
1/3 cup ketchup
1 teaspoon chili powder
1 teaspoon Chinese chili sauce

In a shallow baking dish, combine soy sauce, sherry, chili sauce, sesame oil and cornstarch. Add chicken and stir to coat evenly. Let stand 20 minutes. In a large saucepan of boiling water, cook noodles according to package directions. Drain and set aside.

In a large saucepan of boiling water, cook noodles according to package directions. Drain noodles, turn into a large bowl and toss with 1 tablespoon of the oil. Heat a wok until hot. Add remaining oil and swirl to coat wok. Add garlic, gingerroot and chile and stir-fry 1 minute. Add bell pepper and snow peas and stir-fry 1 minute.

Heat a wok until hot. Add oil and swirl to coat wok. Add celery, mushrooms and bell pepper and stir-fry 3 minutes or until vegetables begin to soften. Add snow peas and green onions and stir-fry 1 minute. Remove to a bowl. Add chicken and marinade to oil remaining in wok. Stir-fry about 3 minutes or until chicken is no longer pink. Add stock and bring to a boil, then add reserved noodles and vegetables and bean sprouts. Stir-fry 2 minutes or until sauce thickens.

Makes 4 to 6 servings.

Add green onions, shrimp and bean sprouts. Stir in ketchup, chili powder, chili sauce and 1/2 cup water. Bring to a boil. Add noodles and stir-fry 2 minutes or until coated with sauce and heated through. Serve hot.

Makes 4 servings.

— VEGETARIAN DISHES & SALADS —

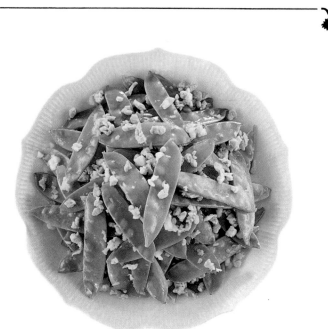

SZECHUAN EGGPLANT

1 pound small eggplants, cut into 1-inch cubes or
    thin slices
Salt
2 tablespoons peanut oil
2 garlic cloves, finely chopped
1-inch piece gingerroot, peeled and finely chopped
3 or 4 green onions, finely sliced
2 tablespoons dark soy sauce
1 or 2 tablespoons hot bean sauce or 1 teaspoon crushed
    dried chiles
1 tablespoon yellow bean paste (optional)
2 tablespoons dry sherry or rice wine
1 tablespoon cider vinegar
1 tablespoon sugar
Chopped parsley, to garnish

STIR-FRIED SNOW PEAS

2 tablespoons vegetable oil
3 garlic cloves, finely chopped
4 ounces lean pork, very finely chopped
1 pound snow peas
1/2 teaspoon crushed palm sugar
1 tablespoon fish sauce
2 ounces cooked peeled shrimp, chopped
Freshly ground pepper

Heat oil in a wok over medium heat, add
garlic and fry until lightly colored. Add pork
and stir-fry 2 to 3 minutes.

Place eggplant cubes in a plastic or stainless
steel colander or sieve, placed on a plate or
baking sheet. Sprinkle with salt and let stand
30 minutes. Rinse eggplant under cold running water and turn out onto layers of paper
towels; pat dry thoroughly. Heat wok until
very hot. Add oil and swirl to coat wok. Add
garlic, gingerroot and green onions and stir-
fry 1 or 2 minutes or until green onions begin
to soften. Add eggplant and stir-fry 2 or 3
minutes or until softened and beginning to
brown.

Add snow peas and stir-fry about 3 minutes
until crisp-tender.

Stir in remaining ingredients and 2/3 cup
water and bring to a boil. Reduce heat and
simmer 5 to 7 minutes or until eggplant is
very tender, stirring frequently. Increase heat
to high and stir-fry mixture until the liquid is
almost completely reduced. Spoon into a
serving dish and garnish with parsley.

Makes 4 to 6 servings.

Stir in sugar, fish sauce, shrimp and pepper.
Heat briefly.

Makes 4 servings.

TOSSED SPINACH

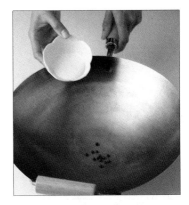

2 tablespoons peanut oil
8 ounces chicken, very finely chopped
6 garlic cloves, finely chopped
1-1/2 pounds spinach leaves, torn into large pieces
1-1/2 tablespoons fish sauce
Freshly ground pepper
1-1/2 tablespoons dry-fried unsalted peanuts, chopped
Thinly sliced fresh red chile, to garnish

Heat oil in a wok, add chicken and stir-fry 2 to 3 minutes. Using a slotted spoon, transfer to paper towels; set aside.

Add garlic to wok and fry until just colored. Using a slotted spoon, transfer 1/2 of the garlic to paper towels; set aside. Increase heat beneath wok so oil is lightly smoking. Quickly add spinach, stir briefly to coat with oil and garlic.

Top spinach with chicken and sprinkle with fish sauce and pepper. Reduce heat, cover wok and simmer 2 to 3 minutes. Scatter peanuts and reserved garlic on top and garnish with sliced chile. Serve immediately.

Makes 4 servings.

SPICED CABBAGE

14 peppercorns
2 tablespoons coconut cream, see page 10
2 shallots, chopped
4 ounces lean pork, finely chopped
About 1 pound white cabbage, finely sliced
1-1/4 cups coconut milk
1 tablespoon fish sauce
1 fresh red chile, very finely chopped

In a wok, heat peppercorns about 3 minutes, until aroma changes. Stir in coconut cream, heat 2 to 3 minutes, then stir in shallots.

Stir-fry 2 to 3 minutes, then stir in pork and cabbage. Cook, stirring occasionally, 3 minutes. Add coconut milk and bring just to a boil. Reduce heat, cover and simmer 5 minutes.

Uncover and cook about 10 minutes until cabbage is crisp-tender. Stir in fish sauce. Sprinkle with chopped chile.

Makes 4 to 5 servings.

VEGETABLES WITH SAUCE

MUSHROOMS & BEAN SPROUTS

1 eggplant (about 8 ounces)
4 ounces long beans or green beans
3 ounces cauliflowerets
2 cups coconut milk
2 shallots, chopped
2 garlic cloves, chopped
4 cilantro roots, chopped
2 dried red chiles, seeded, chopped
2 stalks lemon grass, chopped
1-1/4-inch piece galangal, chopped
Grated peel of 1 lime
1-1/2 tablespoons ground roasted peanuts
3 tablespoons tamarind water, see page 12
1 tablespoon fish sauce
2 teaspoons crushed palm sugar

2 tablespoons vegetable oil
2 fresh red chiles, seeded, thinly sliced
2 garlic cloves, chopped
8 ounces shiitake mushrooms, sliced
4 ounces bean sprouts
4 ounces cooked peeled shrimp
2 tablespoons lime juice
2 shallots, sliced crosswise
1 tablespoon fish sauce
1/2 teaspoon crushed palm sugar
1 tablespoon ground browned rice, see page 12
6 cilantro sprigs, stems and leaves finely chopped
10 Thai mint leaves, shredded
Thai mint leaves to garnish

Cut eggplant into 1-1/2-inch cubes; cut beans into 2-inch lengths. Put all vegetables into a pan, add coconut milk and bring to a boil. Cover and simmer 10 minutes until vegetables are tender. Remove from heat, uncover and set aside. Using a pestle and mortar or small food processor, pound or mix together shallots, garlic, cilantro roots, chiles, lemon grass, galangal and lime peel.

Heat oil in a wok, add chiles and garlic and cook, stirring occasionally, 2 to 3 minutes. Add mushrooms and stir-fry 2 to 3 minutes.

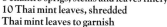

Mix in 1/4 cup liquid from vegetables. Place in a small, heavy skillet, stir in coconut cream and heat, stirring, until the oil separates and paste is thick. Stir into vegetables with peanuts, tamarind water, fish sauce and sugar. Simmer about 1 minute.

Makes 6 servings.

Add bean sprouts and shrimp, stir-fry 1 minute, then stir in lime juice, shallots, fish sauce and sugar. When hot, remove from heat and stir in rice, cilantro and shredded mint. Garnish with mint leaves.

Makes 4 servings.

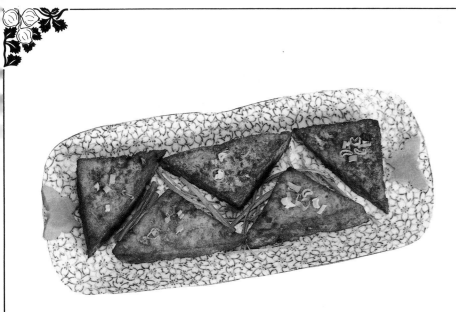

DEEP-FRIED TOFU

1 tablespoon sea salt
1 tablespoon five-spice powder
2 tablespoons sugar
1 teaspoon white pepper
1 garlic clove, very finely chopped
4 tofu cakes, halved (1 pound)
2-1/2 cups peanut oil
4 green onions, very finely chopped

In a bowl, mix together salt, five-spice powder, sugar, pepper and garlic. Add one piece of tofu at a time and turn over to evenly coat. Let stand 1 hour.

In a wok, heat oil until smoking, add tofu and deep-fry 5 minutes until puffy and golden. Drain on paper towels.

Serve immediately sprinkled with the green onions.

Makes 4 servings.

CRISPY SEAWEED

1-3/4 cups tender collard greens or spinach
2-1/2 cups vegetable oil
1 tablespoon brown sugar
1/2 teaspoon sea salt
1/2 teaspoon ground cinnamon
3/4 cup sliced almonds, to garnish, if desired

Remove the thick ribs from the leaves and discard. Wash the leaves, drain and dry thoroughly with paper towels. Using a very sharp knife or cleaver cut the leaves into very fine shreds.

In a wok, heat the oil until smoking, then remove from heat and add greens. Return to medium heat and stir 2 to 3 minutes, or until the shreds begin to float. Using a slotted spoon remove from the oil and drain on paper towels.

In a small bowl, mix together sugar, salt and cinnamon. Place 'seaweed' on a dish and sprinkle with the sugar mixture. Serve cold garnished with sliced almonds, if desired.

Makes 4 servings.

BROCCOLI WITH SHRIMP

3 tablespoons peanut oil
4 garlic cloves, finely chopped
1 red chile, seeded, thinly sliced
1 pound trimmed broccoli, cut diagonally into 1-inch
    slices
4 ounces cooked shrimp
1 tablespoon fish sauce
1/2 teaspoon crushed palm sugar
Chile Flowers, see page 15, to garnish

Heat oil in a wok, add garlic and fry, stirring occasionally, until just beginning to color. Add chile and cook 2 minutes.

Quickly stir in broccoli. Stir-fry 3 minutes. Reduce heat, cover wok and cook 4 to 5 minutes until broccoli is crisp-tender.

Remove lid and stir in shrimp, fish sauce and sugar. Garnish with Chile Flowers.

Makes 4 servings.

BRAISED BAMBOO SHOOTS

1/2 cup cornstarch
1 (15-oz.) can bamboo shoots
2 tablespoons vegetable oil
4 slices gingerroot, peeled
3/4 cup Chinese Chicken Stock, see page 22
1 tablespoon dark soy sauce
1 teaspoon rice wine or dry sherry
1 teaspoon brown sugar
1/2 small red bell pepper, thinly sliced
1/2 small green bell pepper, thinly sliced
1/2 teaspoon sesame oil

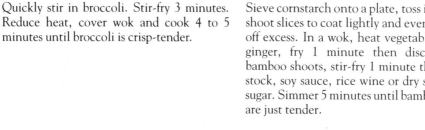

Sieve cornstarch onto a plate, toss in bamboo shoot slices to coat lightly and evenly. Shake off excess. In a wok, heat vegetable oil, add ginger, fry 1 minute then discard. Add bamboo shoots, stir-fry 1 minute then stir in stock, soy sauce, rice wine or dry sherry and sugar. Simmer 5 minutes until bamboo shoots are just tender.

Add bell peppers and cook 3 minutes until softened. Sprinkle with sesame oil.

Makes 4 servings.

SHANGHAI CASSEROLE

1/4 cup peanut oil
1-1/2 cups broccoli flowerets
1 (8-oz.) can bamboo shoots, sliced
1-1/2 cups thinly sliced carrot
8 dried black winter mushrooms, soaked in hot water
    25 minutes, drained, liquid reserved
2 (4-oz.) tofu cakes, cut into bite-sized pieces
2 teaspoons sea salt
1 teaspoon brown sugar
1 tablespoon dark soy sauce
2 tablespoons rice wine or dry sherry
1 teaspoon cornstarch dissolved in 2 teaspoons water

In a saucepan, heat oil, add broccoli, bamboo shoots and carrot, and stir-fry 3 minutes. Stir in mushrooms with their soaking liquid and remaining ingredients except cornstarch mixture and bring to a boil, stirring.

Reduce heat so liquid simmers, cover and cook 15 minutes. If there is too much liquid, stir in cornstarch mixture and heat, stirring until thickened.

Makes 4 servings.

VEGETABLES IN A HAT

1/4 cup Chinese Chicken Stock, see page 22
1 tablespoon rice wine or dry sherry
1/2 teaspoon sea salt
1/2 teaspoon sugar
2 ounces dried wood ear mushrooms, soaked in hot
    water 25 minutes, drained
4 dried black winter mushrooms, soaked in hot water
    25 minutes, drained
4 ounces bean sprouts
1 (3-oz.) can bamboo shoots, drained and finely
    chopped
1-1/4 cups shredded Chinese cabbage
4 ounces bean thread noodles, soaked in hot water 25
    minutes, drained
2 eggs, beaten

In a wok, bring chicken stock, rice wine or dry sherry, salt and sugar to a boil. Stir in mushrooms, bean sprouts, bamboo shoots, cabbage and noodles, then simmer 8 minutes. Drain vegetables and noodles, place in a warmed serving dish and keep warm.

In a skillet, use the eggs to make an omelet. Place the omelet on the vegetables and serve immediately.

Makes 4 servings.

BEAN SALAD

2 tablespoons lime juice
2 tablespoons fish sauce
1/2 teaspoon crushed palm sugar
1-1/2 tablespoons Nam Prik, see page 19
2 tablespoons ground roasted peanuts
2 tablespoons water
2 tablespoons vegetable oil
3 garlic cloves, chopped
3 shallots, thinly sliced
1/4 dried red chile, seeded, finely chopped
2 tablespoons coconut cream, see page 10
8 ounces long beans or green beans, very thinly sliced

In a small bowl, mix together lime juice, fish sauce, sugar, Nam Prik, peanuts and water; set aside. In a small saucepan, heat oil, add garlic and shallots and cook, stirring occasionally, until beginning to brown. Stir in chile and cook until garlic and shallots are browned. Using a slotted spoon, transfer to paper towels; set aside.

In a small saucepan over low heat, warm coconut cream, stirring occasionally. Bring a medium-size saucepan of water to a boil, add beans, return to a boil and cook about 30 seconds. Drain and refresh under cold water. Drain well. Transfer to a serving bowl and toss with shallot mixture and contents of small bowl. Drizzle warm coconut cream over top.

Makes 3 to 4 servings.

SHRIMP SALAD WITH MINT

16 to 20 raw large shrimp, peeled, deveined
Juice of 2 limes
2 teaspoons vegetable oil
2 teaspoons crushed palm sugar
2 tablespoons tamarind water, see page 12
1 tablespoon fish sauce
2 teaspoons Red Curry Paste, see page 18
2 stalks lemon grass, very finely chopped
1/4 cup coconut cream, see page 10
5 kaffir lime leaves, shredded
10 Thai mint leaves, shredded
1 small crisp lettuce head, divided into leaves
1 small cucumber, thinly sliced
Thai mint leaves to garnish

Put shrimp in a bowl, add lime juice and let stand 30 minutes. Remove shrimp, allowing any excess liquid to drain into a bowl; reserve liquid. Heat oil in a wok, add shrimp and stir-fry 2 to 3 minutes until just cooked. (Marinating in lime juice partially cooks them.)

Meanwhile, stir sugar, tamarind water, fish sauce, curry paste, lemon grass, coconut cream, lime leaves and mint leaves into reserved lime liquid. Stir in cooked shrimp. Cover and refrigerate until cold. Line a plate with lettuce; top with a layer of cucumber slices. Spoon shrimp and dressing on top. Garnish with mint leaves.

Makes 3 to 4 servings.

CHICKEN & WATERCRESS

2 garlic cloves, finely chopped
1-1/4-inch piece galangal, finely chopped
1 tablespoon fish sauce
3 tablespoons lime juice
1 teaspoon crushed palm sugar
2 tablespoons peanut oil
8 ounces chicken, very finely chopped
About 25 dried shrimp
1 bunch watercress (about 4 ounces), coarse stalks removed
3 tablespoons chopped roasted peanuts
2 fresh red chiles, seeded, cut into thin strips

CHILE-CHICKEN SALAD

1-1/2 pounds skinless boneless chicken breasts
1-1/4 cups brown rice
3 tablespoons sesame oil
2 tablespoons peanut oil
1 cup cashew nuts or peanuts
5 ounces snow peas
2 tablespoons sunflower oil
1-inch fresh gingerroot, peeled and thinly sliced
2 garlic cloves, finely chopped
4 to 6 green onions, sliced
1 or 2 fresh green chiles, seeded and thinly sliced
3 tablespoons white-wine vinegar
1 tablespoon shredded fresh mint or cilantro
Mixed lettuce leaves
1 orange, peeled, segmented and any juice reserved
Chopped fresh herbs, to garnish

Using a pestle and mortar, pound together garlic and galangal. Mix in fish sauce, lime juice and sugar; set aside. In a wok, heat oil, add chicken and stir-fry about 3 minutes until cooked through. Using a slotted spoon, transfer to paper towels to drain, then put into a serving bowl. Set aside.

Cut chicken into thin strips. Cook rice according to package directions until tender. Drain and place in a large bowl; toss with sesame oil and set aside. Heat a wok until hot, add peanut oil and swirl to coat wok. Add the nuts and stir-fry 1 or 2 minutes or until they turn golden. Remove and add to rice. Add snow peas to oil in wok and stir-fry 1 or 2 minutes or until bright green. Add to the rice. Add chicken strips to wok in 2 batches, and stir-fry 2 or 3 minutes or until chicken turns white and feels firm to the touch. Add to the rice.

Chop half the dried shrimp and add to bowl with chicken. Mix in watercress, peanuts and half of the chiles. Add garlic mixture and toss to mix. Sprinkle with remaining chiles and shrimp.

Makes 3 to 4 servings.

Add sunflower oil to wok and stir in ginger-root, garlic, green onions and chile. Stir-fry 1 minute or until onion begins to soften. Pour contents of wok over rice mixture. Return wok to heat and pour in vinegar, swirling to deglaze wok. Pour vinegar over rice mixture, add mint and toss to mix well. Line a shallow serving bowl with lettuce. Spoon rice mixture over lettuce, decorate with orange segments and pour over any reserved juice. Garnish with chopped herbs.

Makes 4 servings.

THAI BEEF SALAD

12 ounces lean beef, very finely chopped
1-1/2 tablespoons long-grain white rice, browned, coarsely ground, see page 12
1 tablespoon fish sauce
2 tablespoons lime juice
2 teaspoons crushed palm sugar
2 fresh green chiles, seeded, finely chopped
2 garlic cloves, finely chopped
8 Thai mint leaves
4 kaffir lime leaves, torn
8 Thai basil leaves
Lettuce leaves to serve
Chopped green onions and a Chili Flower, see page 15, to garnish

PORK & BAMBOO SHOOT SALAD

3 tablespoons vegetable oil
3 garlic cloves, chopped
1 small onion, thinly sliced
8 ounces lean pork, very finely chopped
1 egg, beaten
1 (8-oz.) can bamboo shoots, drained, cut into strips
1 tablespoon fish sauce
1 teaspoon crushed palm sugar
3 tablespoons lime juice
Freshly ground pepper
Lettuce leaves to serve
Fried garlic and onion to garnish

Heat a wok, add beef and dry-fry about 2 minutes until no longer pink. Transfer to a bowl. In a small bowl, mix together ground rice, fish sauce, lime juice and sugar. Pour over warm beef and toss together. Cover and cool until slightly warm.

In a wok, heat 2 tablespoons of the oil, add garlic and onion and cook, stirring occasionally, until lightly browned. Using a slotted spoon, transfer to paper towels to drain; set aside. Add pork to wok and stir-fry about 3 minutes until cooked through. Using a slotted spoon, transfer to paper towels; set aside. Using paper towels, wipe out wok.

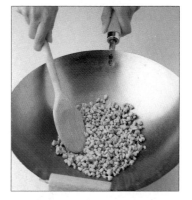

Add chiles, garlic and mint, lime leaves and basil leaves to bowl and toss ingredients together. Line a plate with lettuce leaves; spoon beef mixture into center. Top with green onions and garnish with Chile Flower.

Makes 3 to 4 servings.

Heat remaining oil in wok, pour in egg to make a thin layer and cook 1 to 2 minutes until just set. Turn over and cook 1 minute. Remove, roll up and cut into strips. In a bowl, toss together pork, bamboo shoots and egg. In a small bowl, stir together fish sauce, sugar, lime juice and plenty of pepper. Pour over pork mixture and toss. Line a plate with lettuce leaves; spoon pork mixture into center. Sprinkle with fried garlic and onion.

Makes 3 to 4 servings.

DESSERTS

PEKING APPLES

CHINESE FRUIT SOUP

1 egg
1/2 cup water
1 cup all-purpose flour
4 crisp eating apples
2-1/2 cups vegetable oil
SYRUP:
1 tablespoon vegetable oil
2 tablespoons water
6 tablespoons brown sugar
2 tablespoons corn syrup
Iced water to set

In a large bowl, stir the egg and water into the flour to make a thick batter.

1/2 cup rice wine or dry sherry
Juice and peel of 2 limes
3-1/2 cups water
1 cup sugar
1 piece lemon grass
4 whole cloves
2-inch cinnamon stick
1 vanilla bean, split
Pinch ground nutmeg
1 teaspoon coriander seeds, lightly crushed
1-1/2 to 2-inch piece gingerroot, peeled and thinly
    sliced
1/4 cup raisins
1 pound prepared fresh fruits, eg. mango, strawberries,
    lychees, star fruit, kiwi fruit

Peel, core and thickly slice apples. Dip each apple slice in the batter to evenly coat; allow excess to drain off. In a wok, heat oil until smoking. Add apple pieces in batches and deep-fry 3 minutes until golden brown. Using a slotted spoon, remove to paper towels to drain.

In a saucepan, place rice wine or dry sherry, lime juice and peel, water, sugar, lemon grass, cloves, cinnamon, vanilla, nutmeg, coriander and gingerroot. Heat gently, stirring until sugar dissolves, then bring to a boil. Reduce heat and simmer 5 minutes. Cool, then strain into a bowl. Add raisins, then chill.

To make syrup, in a small saucepan, gently heat oil, water and sugar, stirring until sugar has dissolved. Simmer 5 minutes, stirring. Stir in corn syrup and boil 5 to 10 minutes until thick and syrupy. Reduce heat to very low. Dip each piece of apple into syrup to coat then place in ice-cold water a few seconds. Remove to a serving dish. Repeat with remaining apple. Serve immediately.

Makes 4 servings.

Arrange a selection of prepared fruit in 4 individual serving dishes and spoon syrup over.

Makes 4 servings.

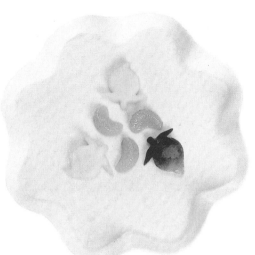

EXOTIC MANGO MOUSSE

1 (14-oz.) can mandarin orange sections, drained
1 (14-oz.) can mango pulp
1-3/4 cups whipping cream
3 tablespoons unflavored gelatin powder
1/3 cup water
4 egg whites
3 tablespoons brown sugar

Reserve a few mandarin sections. In a food processor or blender, process the remaining oranges until smooth, pour into a measuring jug and add water to make 3 cups.

Turn into a large bowl; stir in mango pulp. In a bowl, beat cream until soft peaks form. Fold into mango mixture until just evenly combined. In a small bowl, sprinkle gelatin over water, let soften 5 minutes, then place bowl over a saucepan of boiling water. Stir until gelatin dissolves then remove bowl from heat and cool slightly. Stir in a little of the remaining mango mixture, then stir into the large bowl; chill until almost set.

In a clean bowl, beat egg whites until soft peaks form then beat in sugar. Carefully fold into mango mixture until just evenly mixed. Serve in individual dishes decorated with the reserved mandarins sections.

Makes 8 servings.

COCONUT CREPES

4 ounces rice flour
1/3 cup sugar
Pinch of salt
1-3/4 cups shredded coconut
2 eggs, beaten
2-1/2 cups coconut milk
Green food coloring and red food coloring, if desired
Vegetable oil for cooking
Tangerine sections, to serve, if desired

In a bowl, stir together rice flour, sugar, salt and coconut.

Form a well in center, add eggs, then gradually draw in flour mixture, slowly pouring in coconut milk at same time, to make a smooth batter. If desired, divide batter evenly among 3 bowls. Stir green food coloring into one bowl to color batter pale green; color another batch pink and leave remaining batch plain. Heat a 6-inch crepe or omelet pan over medium heat, swirl around a little oil, then pour off excess. Stir batter well, then add 2 to 3 spoonfuls to pan.

Rotate to cover bottom, then cook over medium heat about 4 minutes until lightly browned underneath and set. Carefully turn over and cook briefly on other side. Transfer to a warmed plate and keep warm while cooking remaining batter. Serve rolled up with tangerine sections, if using.

Makes about 10.

Note: The mixture is delicate so the first 2 or 3 crepes may be difficult to make perfectly.

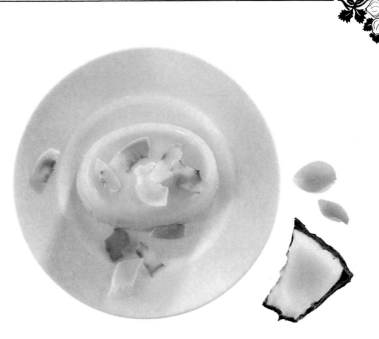

MANGO WITH STICKY RICE

COCONUT CUSTARDS

1-1/4 cups sticky rice, soaked overnight in cold water
1 cup coconut milk
Pinch of salt
2 to 4 tablespoons sugar or to taste
2 large ripe mangoes, peeled and halved
3 tablespoons coconut cream, see page 10
Mint leaves to decorate

2 egg yolks
3 eggs
2 cups coconut milk
1/3 cup sugar
Few drops rosewater or jasmine extract
Toasted coconut to decorate

Drain and rinse rice thoroughly. Place in a steaming basket lined with a double thickness of cheesecloth. Steam over simmering water 30 minutes. Remove from heat.

Preheat oven to 350F (175C). Place 4 individual heatproof custard cups in a baking pan.

In a medium-size bowl, stir together coconut milk, salt and sugar to taste until sugar has dissolved. Stir in warm rice. Set aside 30 minutes.

In a medium-size bowl, stir together egg yolks, eggs, coconut milk, sugar and rosewater or jasmine extract until sugar dissolves. Pour through a strainer into cups. Pour boiling water into baking pan to surround cups.

Thinly slice mangoes by cutting lengthwise through flesh to the seed. Discard the seeds. Spoon rice into mounds in centers of 4 plates and arrange mango slices around. Pour coconut cream over rice. Decorate with mint leaves.

Makes 4 servings.

Bake about 20 minutes until a knife inserted off-center in custard comes out clean. Remove from baking pan and cool slightly before unmolding. Serve warm or cold. Decorate with toasted coconut.

Makes 4 servings.

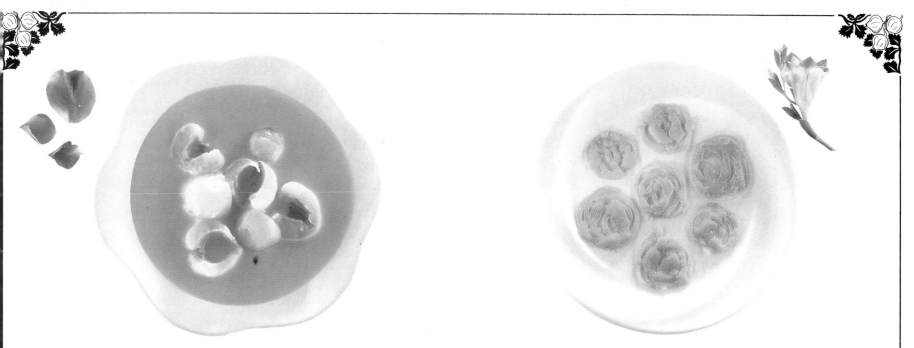

LYCHEES IN COCONUT CUSTARD

GOLDEN THREADS

3 egg yolks
3 to 4 tablespoons sugar
Scant 1 cup coconut milk
1/3 cup coconut cream, see page 10
About 1 tablespoon triple-distilled rose water
Red food coloring
About 16 fresh lychees, peeled, halved and seeds removed
Rose petals, to decorate

6 egg yolks
1 teaspoon egg white
2 cups sugar
Few drops of jasmine extract
1 cup water

In a bowl, beat together egg yolks and sugar until light.

Strain egg yolks through cheesecloth into a small bowl. Beat lightly with egg white. In a saucepan, gently heat sugar, jasmine extract and water, stirring until sugar dissolves, then boil until thickened slightly. Adjust heat so syrup is hot but not moving.

In a medium-size nonstick saucepan, heat coconut milk to just below boiling, then slowly stir into sugar mixture. Return to pan and cook over low heat, stirring with a wooden spoon, until custard coats the back of the spoon.

Spoon a small amount of egg yolk mixture into a pastry bag fitted with a tip with a very small hole or a cone of waxed paper with a very small hole in the pointed end. Using a circular movement, carefully dribble a trail of egg into syrup, making swirls about 1-1/2 to 2 inches in diameter with a small hole in center. Make a few at a time, cooking each briefly until set.

Remove from heat and stir in coconut cream, rose water to taste and enough red food coloring to color pale pink. Refrigerate until cold, stirring occasionally. Spoon a thin layer of custard into 4 small bowls. Arrange lychees on custard. Decorate with rose petals. Serve remaining custard separately to pour over lychees.

Makes 4 servings.

Using a skewer inserted in the hole in the center of the spiral, transfer each nest to a plate. Continue making similar nests with the remaining egg yolk mixture. When nests are cool, arrange on a clean plate.

Makes 4 servings.

INDEX